E-Learning in the 21st Century

D1013929

The second edition of *E-Learning in the 21st Century* provides a coherent, comprehensive, and empirically-based framework for understanding e-learning in higher education. The author draws on his decades of experience and extensive research in the field to explore the technological, pedagogical, and organizational implications of e-learning. Most importantly, he provides practical models that educators can use to realize the full potential of e-learning. This book is unique in that it focuses less on the long list of ever-evolving technologies and more on the search for an understanding of these technologies from an educational perspective.

This second edition has been fully revised and updated throughout and includes discussions of social media and mobile learning applications as well as other emerging technologies in today's classrooms. This book is an invaluable resource for courses on e-learning in higher education as well as for researchers, practitioners, and senior administrators looking for guidance on how to successfully adopt e-learning in their institutions.

Dr. D. Randy Garrison is the Director of the Teaching & Learning Centre and a professor in the Faculty of Education at the University of Calgary. He is the author of eight books, including *Blended Learning in Higher Education* (2008) and *An Introduction to Distance Education: Understanding Teaching and Learning in a New Era* (2010). Dr. Garrison was the recipient of the 2009 Sloan-C Award for Most Outstanding Achievement in Online Learning by an Individual.

E-Learning in the 21st Century

A Framework for Research and Practice

Second Edition

D. Randy Garrison

Routledge
Taylor & Francis Group

NEW YORK AND LONDON

First edition published 2003

This edition published 2011–
by Routledge
270 Madison Avenue, New York, NY 10016

Simultaneously published in the UK
by Routledge
2 Park Square, Milton Park, Abingdon, Oxon OX14 4RN

Routledge is an imprint of the Taylor & Francis Group, an informa business

Typeset in Sabon
by Keystroke, Station Road, Codsall, Wolverhampton
Printed and bound in the United States of America on acid-free paper
by Walsworth Publishing Company, Marceline, MO

Library of Congress Cataloging in Publication Data
Garrison, D. R. (D. Randy), 1945–
    E-learning in the 21st century : a framework for research and practice /
D.R. Garrison. — 2nd ed.
        p. cm.
    Includes bibliographical references and index.
    1. Education, Higher—Computer network resources. 2. Education, Higher—
Effect of technological innovations on. 3. Internet in higher education.
4. Distance education. I. Title. II. Title: E-learning in the twenty-first century.
    LB2395.7.G37 2011+
    070.9′09051—dc22   2010036587

ISBN13: 978–0–415–88582–9 (hbk)
ISBN13: 978–0–415–88583–6 (pbk)
ISBN13: 978–0–203–83876–1 (ebk)

SUSTAINABLE
FORESTRY
INITIATIVE

Certified Sourcing
www.sfiprogram.org

The SFI label applies to the text stock.

Contents

List of Illustrations

Preface to the Second Edition

The goal of the second edition of *E-Learning in the 21st Century* is to provide an update based on a decade of research since the first publication of the Community of Inquiry framework (Garrison, Anderson & Archer, 2000). The first edition essentially compiled the original set of articles authored by the principle researchers. In the second edition, Chapters 1, 4 and 12 have been completely rewritten, a new chapter has been added (Chapter 8) and the remaining chapters have undergone significant revision to incorporate the considerable research of an e-learning community of inquiry since the first publication. The revisions provide new perspectives and understanding that enhance considerably the Community of Inquiry framework as a theoretical and practical guide.

This book is an inquiry into e-learning in higher education. By inquiry we mean the process of transforming an "indeterminate situation" into one that is unified and coherent—to paraphrase Dewey (1938, p. 117). The primary product of this inquiry has been the Community of Inquiry theoretical framework. The framework has also provided guidance in the subsequent inquiry into e-learning. While this may sound like a closed loop, true inquiry is open to new evidence and insights; and there have been many insights over the years that we will explore in this new edition.

I do want to express how grateful and indebted I am to all those who believed in and contributed to the development of the Community of Inquiry (CoI) framework since the publication of the original articles. There is a core group of researchers who have formed a very productive community, have provided important insights, and have been instrumental in moving the CoI framework to becoming a credible theory for e-learning. In this regard, I wish to acknowledge and sincerely thank the following for their support, ideas, and belief in this work: Zehra Akyol, Ben Arbaugh, Marti Cleveland-Innes, Sebastian Diaz, Phil Ice, Jennifer Richardson, Peter Shea, Karen Swan, and Norm Vaughan. In particular, I want to thank former doctoral students of mine Norm Vaughan and Zehra Akyol, for their friendship and for keeping me immersed in research associated with the CoI framework. Of course, I remain indebted to my colleagues Terry Anderson and Walter Archer for their creative contributions to the original CoI framework. Finally, I must also acknowledge the many other researchers and graduate students that have used and contributed to the development of the CoI framework and the acceptance of online and blended learning in higher education.

It has been an exciting and fulfilling journey and I hope there will be further adventures as we move into the second decade of this research. I feel we have just begun to take flight as e-learning and the CoI theoretical framework enter the mainstream of higher education.

D. Randy Garrison
January, 2011

Preface to the First Edition

The goal of *E-Learning in the 21st Century* is to provide a framework for understanding the application of e-learning in higher education. We view e-learning as that learning facilitated online through network technologies. This does not preclude any number of other technologies or approaches, including components of face-to-face educational experiences. However, we will confine our discussion to those learning activities conducted through electronic means online.

Various authors have described the growth of e-learning as explosive, unprecedented, amazing, and disruptive. In fact, there are those who argue that we are experiencing a revolution in higher education (Report of a University of Illinois Faculty Seminar, 1999). Others suggest that e-learning technology is unique (Harasim, 1989) and represents a new era of distance education (Garrison, 1997a). Regardless of the rhetoric, what has changed is the "speed and power of communications and the expanded capacity to send, receive, and use information" (Ikenberry, 1999, p. 57) and the capacity to bridge time and space for educational purposes.

While lifelong learning has become an imperative, and communications technologies are transforming higher education, in most instances "the revolution proceeds without any clear vision or master plan" (Ikenberry, 1999: 58). Considering the massive adoption of e-learning, what is surprising, and cause for concern, is that we know so little about the use of this medium to facilitate learning (Gilbert, 2000). To date, published research and guides consist of innumerable case studies and personal descriptions and prescriptions but little in the way of rigorous, research-based constructs that lead to an in-depth understanding of e-learning in higher education.

Considering the ubiquity of e-learning, and the enormous opportunities and risks that it presents for higher education, we need more than a fragmented approach to studying and understanding this phenomenon. Is e-learning to be used simply to enhance inherently deficient existing practices (e.g., lecturing)? Or does this technology have the potential to transform the educational transaction towards the ideal of a community of inquiry?

Such questions can only be addressed and explored through empirically based research frameworks like those presented in this book.

HOW THE BOOK CAME TO BE

The authors will provide educators with a deep understanding of the characteristics of e-learning. This in-depth understanding will give direction and guidance to educators who wish to facilitate critical discourse and higher-order learning through the use of electronic technologies in a networked learning context. All universities and colleges now have large numbers of faculty members using e-learning to enhance their campus-based and distance-education programming. Some of the most innovative technological e-learning approaches are being built in corporations to improve performance and retain competitive advantages.

OVERVIEW OF CONTENTS

The first chapter describes the context and outlines the challenges of exploring and understanding the potential of e-learning. It makes the point that e-learning is not just another learning technology. There is every reason to believe it will transform teaching and learning.

The second chapter outlines the philosophical perspective and theoretical concepts that frame our understanding of e-learning. It also outlines a set of principles that guide a deep and meaningful approach to e-learning.

The third chapter speaks to the organizing concept for realizing the potential of e-learning. The Community of Inquiry model is the conceptual framework that defines the three constituting elements of e-learning—social, cognitive, and teaching presence. This conceptual model takes us back to the roots and core values of higher education. We then discuss the place of technology in this learning community.

The fourth chapter provides an overview of technology and its development. The impact of the Internet as well as the role and nature of interaction in e-learning is then discussed.

The fifth chapter explores the challenge of creating a climate for higher-order learning in an e-learning environment. Categories, indicators, and suggestions that have practical value in establishing social presence are provided.

The sixth chapter offers an analysis and model of critical thinking and practical inquiry for cognitive presence. From this, descriptors and indicators for each of the phases of practical inquiry are described. This provides insights into the cognitive dimensions of e-learning.

The seventh chapter completes the Community of Inquiry model with a discussion of teaching presence and its central function in e-learning. Categories and indicators of teaching presence are outlined and practical implications for structuring, facilitating, and directing are addressed.

The eighth chapter shifts to the practical issues of implementing e-learning. It begins by discussing the purposes and strengths of various learning activities. The rest of the chapter approaches e-learning from the perspective of teaching presence and its dimensions but focusing on issues of social and cognitive presence. Guidelines and specific suggestions for practice are provided.

The ninth chapter addresses assessment and evaluation that is arguably the most influential element of any educational experience. Assessment of e-learning goes beyond judging student performance. Assessment of the development and delivery of e-learning is also necessary to advance our understanding of meaningful and worthwhile learning.

The tenth chapter moves out of the classroom to consider institutional issues to prepare for e-learning in the twenty-first century. The chapter explores the dynamics of change and the need for leadership, policy, and infrastructure with regard to innovation and the strategic integration of e-learning in institutions of higher education.

The last chapter provides an imaginative look into the future with regard to e-learning. Its unique properties are described and a glimpse into the future provided.

CONTRIBUTION

The early chapters demonstrate that e-learning can create asynchronous communities of inquiry which have the potential to support the development of collaborative communities of learning, while still allowing "anytime, anywhere" access by students. We are convinced that such technology, when combined with effective pedagogy and reflective teaching, will transform higher education. In the later chapters of the book, this potential is translated into practical guidelines intended to be used by educators working to realize the full potential of e-learning.

This book contributes a meaningful framework and approach to the understanding of the fundamentals of e-learning and explains why it is proliferating throughout a rapidly evolving learning society. This is the first comprehensive and coherent framework to guide our understanding of e-learning in higher education and society.

To this point, communications technologies have been driving the unprecedented growth of e-learning. The focus in this book is less on the specifics of the ever-evolving technologies used for e-learning, and more on the search for a deep understanding of these technologies from an educational perspective. It is to the purpose of mapping the territory of e-learning, then providing directional choices for higher education and specific guidelines to reach worthwhile destinations, that this book makes its contribution.

This book is of particular relevance to those who are less impressed with technological gadgetry but who have been waiting for a strong pedagogical reason to participate in the paradigm shift in teaching and learning that e-learning represents. This book will appeal to a broad audience interested in e-learning. The primary audiences, however, are researchers, practitioners, and senior administrators in higher education who must guide the adoption in their institutions of this unique and rapidly proliferating technology.

This book can be used as a basic research framework and tool to study and understand the characteristics of e-learning and to explore its optimal educational applications. It will also be useful as a textbook for adult education and training as well as any number of instructional-technology and distance-education courses. Finally, it will be a valuable reference and guide for senior decision-makers in higher education.

Acknowledgments

The research on which this book is based originated most directly from a major research grant which allowed the author to study the characteristics and qualities of e-learning, with specific reference to the ability of e-learning to foster higher-order learning. It also represented the culmination of years of experience in this field by the original researchers who have brought to the project a broad range of different but complementary perspectives and expertise gained through their teaching and learning experiences and original research.

Chapter 1

Introduction

Pedagogical and technological innovations are redefining higher education. At the nexus of this convergence is e-learning. Concurrent quality and cost reduction pressures are creating the conditions for the transformation of higher education. The ubiquitous and cost-effective technologies used to access information and connect learners have significantly shifted thinking in higher education. At the core of this shift in thinking is the idea that students should be actively engaged in sustainable communities of inquiry. It has been shown that active engagement in a learning community is associated with reflective discourse and deep learning outcomes (Akyol & Garrison, in press a; Brown, 2001; Chapman, Ramondt, & Smiley, 2005; Rovai, 2002). The point has been made that if e-learning approaches "do not deepen the learning experiences of students, they are not worth much" (Weigel, 2002, p. 1). The affordances of new, ubiquitous and powerful communications technologies and their ability to create and sustain communities of learners have quietly established e-learning in the mainstream of higher education.

It is the convergence of the technological and pedagogical developments that is driving e-learning innovation in higher education and the focus of *E-Learning in the 21st Century*. This book provides a coherent understanding of e-learning and how the possibilities are transforming approaches to teaching and learning. E-learning is described here from an educational perspective and its collaborative potential to create and sustain a community of learners. In the context of a rapidly changing knowledge society, it is essential to evolve the learning experience in a way that models and prepares students for an active and collaborative working life. The greatest mistake is to try to integrate new communications technology into passive educational approaches. E-learning will fail if we merely add on to or repackage our current educational designs. We must be prepared to rethink current dominant approaches and be clear as to what type of learning experiences we wish to design. This will require a theoretical framework and models to guide our study and application of e-learning in higher education. However, before we can explore such a framework we need to be clear as to what we mean by e-learning.

E-LEARNING DESCRIBED

The term e-learning came into use in the mid-1990s along with developments in the World Wide Web and interest in asynchronous discussion groups. The goal of e-learning described here is to create a community of inquiry independent of time and location through the use of information and communications technology. An educational community of inquiry is a group of individuals who collaboratively engage in purposeful critical discourse and reflection to construct personal meaning and confirm mutual understanding. This perspective, of course, reflects a particular educational approach using the possibilities of new and emerging technologies to build collaborative constructivist learning communities.

E-learning is formally defined as electronically mediated asynchronous and synchronous communication for the purpose of constructing and confirming knowledge. The technological foundation of e-learning is the Internet and associated communication technologies. Beyond the general description of e-learning, the two primary applications that constitute e-learning are online and blended learning. Fully online learning is a form of distance education that had its genesis apart from mainstream distance education. However, because of its interactive nature, online learning is very different from traditional distance education with its historical focus on content delivery and independent learning. On the other hand, blended learning is the most prevalent form of e-learning in traditional higher education institutions. Somewhat counter-intuitively, the reality is that much of "e-learning innovation has taken place on-campus" (*E-learning in Tertiary Education*, 2005, p. 69). E-learning in the context of blended learning has shifted the thinking of educators in higher education in terms of transformative course and program redesign.

As alluded to previously, e-learning is not an industrialized form of distance education. E-learning in higher education is first and foremost about providing a quality educational experience. While e-learning has an element of distance education, it has evolved from a different field of theory and practice. Distance has become but a relatively minor structural constraint in providing a quality, highly interactive learning experience. E-learning represents a true paradigm shift with regard to distance education. It represents a shift from the ideal of autonomy and the industrial production of prepackaged study materials characteristic of mainstream distance education. E-learning represents a distinct educational branch with its roots in computer conferencing and collaborative constructivist approaches to learning.

This shift in pedagogical assumptions and approaches reflected in the theory and practice of e-learning is a new era of distance education. E-learning in the form of online learning represents the post-industrial era of distance education marked by a return to a craft model of designing context-specific collaborative educational experiences (Garrison & Cleveland-Innes,

2010). Online learning integrates independence (asynchronous online communication) with interaction (connectivity) that overcomes time and space constraints in a way that emulates the values of higher education. In particular, online learning goes beyond the technology and tools to access information. The focus is shifted to the educational transaction in the form of a virtual community of learners sustainable across time (Garrison, 2009a).

At the same time, for e-learning to be fully integrated in the mainstream of higher education, we must not undermine or discount the enormous value of face-to-face educational experience. E-learning should not be viewed as replacing these experiences. Nor should we, however, ignore or resist the obvious advantages of e-learning technologies to access information and sustain educational discourse. The integration of e-learning technologies should not be seen as creating winners and losers. The power of blending online and face-to-face experiences is that it respects the distinct advantages and preferences associated with face-to-face learning communities while recognizing and integrating the enormous strengths of online learning to provide sustained, rigorous discourse.

The potential of e-learning to merge verbal and written discourse, unconstrained by time, has caused educators to rethink the possibilities for engaging campus-based students in face-to-face and online environments. This thoughtful blending of complementary face-to-face and online approaches to meet specific educational goals has been termed blended learning (Garrison & Vaughan, 2008). E-learning in the form of blended learning integrates the best features of online and face-to-face education. Blended learning, however, is not benign. It will inherently precipitate a fundamental rethinking and questioning of current approaches to teaching and learning. Approaches such as the lecture are critically examined in terms of its ability to engage students in critical discourse.

To this point, e-learning has been described in terms of online and blended learning. It has also been argued that e-learning is not a synonym for distance education. With the proliferation of Internet technologies, distance has become relatively meaningless. In an e-learning scenario communities of learners are able to sustain themselves productively across time and space and be enriched immeasurably through the Internet. But this does not just happen by adopting e-learning technologies. It is the ideas that drive this vision, and the core concept here is the community of inquiry. It is this vision and theoretical framework that provide the principles and guidelines that make e-learning a viable reality in higher education.

A NEW REALITY

E-learning is not simply another technological innovation that fundamentally has little impact on the educational experience. With the power of the WWW, the teaching and learning transaction is exposed to unfathomable amounts of information. E-learning is an open system that blends access to information and purposeful communication into a dynamic and intellectually challenging learning community. E-learning transforms education in ways that extend beyond efficient delivery or entertainment value. It is not issues of access to information but the connection to others that distinguishes e-learning from both conventional face-to-face or distance education. Surfing the Internet is not an educational experience, any more than wandering through a library is, and it is disingenuous to acknowledge it as anything more than informal learning.

Not long ago, the provision of increased learner independence in terms of space and time meant a corresponding loss of collaboration and increased isolation. Independence and interaction were inherently contradictory in an educational context—more of one meant less of the other. The transformational power of e-learning goes to the heart of this issue. E-learning has the potential to fully integrate the benefits of personal freedom with connectivity (belonging to a purposeful group of learners). From an educational perspective the "e" in e-learning stands for more than electronic; it can also stand for extending and enhancing the learning experience. It is how we take advantage of e-learning's educational properties and potential that is of greatest interest. This will be more fully explored in subsequent chapters related to collaborative constructive learning and critical reflection and discourse.

To realize the potential of e-learning as an open but cohesive system, it is essential that we rethink our pedagogy. Education is about ideas, not isolated bits of information. With its large lecture halls and standardized, objective testing, higher education has taken on an industrial character. Higher education institutions are addressing their financial challenges by increasing class sizes without addressing quality issues. E-learning's transformative power and capacity to add value is based upon better ways to make sense of the access to unbelievable amounts of information. The current passive information-transfer approaches of higher education are contrasted with the interactive and constructive potential of e-learning.

While e-learning can support and even marginally enhance current practices, such as lecturing, the real impact will be to precipitate new approaches that recognize and seize e-learning's collaborative potential. In reality, this may well be a back-to-the-future scenario as we return to educational experiences founded in communities of inquiry. A community of inquiry is where individual experiences and ideas are recognized and discussed in light of societal knowledge, norms, and values. An e-learning community of inquiry is where autonomy and collaboration are not contradictory ideas but the essential elements of a unified and qualitative shift in how we approach higher education.

In the mid-1980s, the personal computer became accessible to a large and growing number of people. Today, it is the interface to the Internet and the

WWW that is transforming teaching and learning. We are just beginning to discover and understand the extent to which these technologies will transform expectations for, and approaches to, learning. These technologies do not represent more of the same. With the ubiquity of communications technologies and their multiple forms (e.g., text, visual, voice) we are in the early stages of a true educational revolution. The application that is having the greatest influence on education is e-learning.

Although e-learning has attracted much attention, its adoption has largely outstripped our understanding of the technology from an educational perspective. Its value is not faster access to information, or even information itself. The value of e-learning is its capacity to support communication and thinking in the quest to construct meaning and confirm knowledge. Upon reflection, it should be no surprise that most research into using technology for educational purposes has shown no significant differences in learning outcomes between traditional and technically advanced media. Why would we expect to find significant differences if we do essentially the same thing we always have done except change the medium of communication?

Higher education institutions are moving beyond infatuation with the technology and are beginning to address the real challenges of providing a relevant and quality education experience. It is the recognition of the possibilities of e-learning to create and sustain these learning communities that is transforming higher education.

CONCLUSION

E-learning does not represent more of the same. Communication technologies, with their multiple media (text, visual, voice) and their capacity to extend interaction over time and distance, are transforming teaching and learning. The adoption of e-learning applications in the last decade has been accompanied by an increased understanding of how to use them to enhance the educational experience in a cost-effective manner. This book is dedicated to increasing the awareness and understanding of e-learning to enhance a worthwhile educational experience.

However, the challenge is enormous and there are no simple rules or recipes for designing and delivering an effective e-learning experience. The complexities of context and distinct communication characteristics to support communities of inquiry do not lend themselves to easy or simplistic solutions. Any educational experience demands the experience and insight of a reflective and knowledgeable teacher who can translate principles and guidelines to the contingencies and exigencies of their unique contexts. This necessitates an inquisitive attitude and commitment to the process of inquiry not dissimilar to the goals of higher education and the approach described here.

In realistically addressing the complexities of e-learning, the intent is to provide conceptual order along with principles and guidelines that have generalizability and value for educators. Therefore, the challenge for the reader is to make sense of the ideas presented here by translating the concepts and ideas and applying them pragmatically to their unique educational context. This book is about doing things differently. We need to start by asking what e-learning will allow us to do that we could not do before. It is not about entrenching deficient face-to-face approaches such as lecturing by using e-learning to access more irrelevant or incomprehensible information. Nor is it about having students experience the same deficient educational approaches through a different medium.

We find ourselves no further ahead because the regressive activities mentioned above have defined the *status quo* and reinforced a defensive strategy. Marshall McLuhan (1995) argued that the content of a new media is initially always an older media. Thus, the first use of cinema was to record plays and the first use of the Internet was mail. Likewise, the first educational application of the Internet was to disseminate lectures and replace paper syllabi. Now, however, we are challenged to go beyond these early adaptations and develop educational approaches that exploit the possibilities of e-learning to support sustainable communities of inquiry.

Increasingly, higher education is returning to its roots by focusing on the values and practices associated with collaborative approaches to learning. This is a distinct reaction to the dominant individual and isolating approaches to learning that have evolved for fiscal reasons in the last few decades. Perhaps it is time to recast the educational dinosaur and utilize the technologies of e-learning to move away from the transmission modality. Education is but an illusion if it simply disseminates information without actively supporting a critical assessment and the opportunity to construct meaningful knowledge structures that will serve future learning challenges. The goal here is not simply to advocate or promote the use of e-learning. The real challenge and benefit is to understand the nature and potential of e-learning and its implications for a collaborative and constructive educational experience.

Part I

The Conceptual Framework

Chapter 2

Theoretical Foundations

A theoretical foundation for teaching and learning will reflect fundamental values and beliefs about an educational experience. It is by making explicit the theoretical elements that we reveal our educational ideals that will have a profound influence on practice. When adopting new communication technologies with the potential to fundamentally alter the teaching and learning transaction, it is essential we think through our educational ideals. E-learning has become the protagonist for change in higher education, but the plot needs a purpose and direction.

The goal of this chapter is to outline the assumptions, themes, concepts, and principles that underpin the theoretical framework for e-learning in higher education. The fundamental questions addressed are associated with the nature of a worthwhile higher education experience.

PHILOSOPHICAL PERSPECTIVE

While e-learning will most certainly be the dominant approach in supporting new approaches to teaching and learning, sound educational principles must inevitably create the foundation for these innovations if we are to realize meaningful and worthwhile learning outcomes. However, before exploring specific concepts and principles, it is important briefly to explicate the educational assumptions that have shaped the framework described in subsequent chapters.

The foundational perspective of this book reflects a "collaborative constructivist" view of teaching and learning. It is recognition of the inseparable relationship between personal meaning making and the social influence in shaping the educational transaction (Garrison & Archer, 2000). This unified process recognizes the interplay between individual meaning and socially redeeming knowledge. More specifically, collaboration and constructivism correspond respectively to teaching and learning responsibilities in an educational experience. The teaching and learning transaction is a coherent representation and translation of the dynamics of a collaborative and constructive educational experience. The recognition of these two interests is crucial in constructing a theoretical framework through which we can understand and apply e-learning for educational purposes.

Philosophically, this collaborative constructivist perspective is associated with the work of John Dewey. Dewey (1938) identified the principle of "interaction" which unifies the subjective (personal) and objective (social) worlds in an immediate timeframe. Through this interaction, ideas are generated that illuminate the external world. That is, meaning is constructed and shared. Through interaction, ideas are communicated and knowledge is constructed and confirmed. Dewey rejected all dualistic thinking—particularly with regard to the individual and society. For Dewey, society and the individual cannot exist separately, nor can one be subordinated to the other (Dewey & Childs, 1981). To understand education is to understand this interplay between personal interests and experience, and societal values, norms, and knowledge. This interplay is manifest in the transaction between teacher and student.

Dewey's concept of an activity-based education describes an educational experience as a "transaction taking place between an individual and what, at the time, constitutes his environment . . ." (1938, p. 43). For Dewey, transactional communication is the defining component of the educational experience when students transform the inert information passed to them from another and construct it into knowledge with personal application and value (Dewey, 1916). Dewey's description fits with the complex shifting of time and place that defines e-learning and further emphasizes the importance of communication with the various human participants and through the technologies that constitute the environment.

A TRANSACTIONAL VIEW

While knowledge is a social artifact, in an educational context it is the individual learner who must grasp its meaning or offer an improved understanding. The purposeful process of facilitating an outcome that is both socially and personally worthwhile goes to the heart of the teaching and learning transaction. This transaction is common to all educational experiences, including e-learning.

Thus, an educational experience has a dual purpose. The first is to construct meaning (reconstruction of experience) from a personal perspective. The second is to refine and confirm this understanding collaboratively within a community of learners. At first glance, this dual purpose would seem to reflect, respectively, the distinct perspectives of the teacher and student. However, closer consideration of the transaction reveals the inseparability of the teaching and learning roles and the importance of viewing the educational process as a unified transaction. We are simply viewing the same process from two different perspectives. Teachers are learners and learners are teachers. These two perspectives raise fundamental questions concerning issues of responsibility for learning and control of the process.

Responsibility and Control

In an educational transaction, issues of responsibility and control apply to both teaching and learning. The responsibilities of the teacher are complex in that they create and shape the evolving learning environment. This challenge becomes more daunting when powerful technologies are introduced. Educators must create the cognitive and social conditions that will allow and encourage students to approach learning in a meaningful way. While this demands content expertise, it is what the teacher does pedagogically that determines the degree to which students assume responsibility for their learning. Having the learner accept responsibility for one's learning is a crucial step in realizing successful educational outcomes—both in terms of specific knowledge structures and in terms of developing the higher-order cognitive abilities that are necessary for higher-order continuous learning.

Issues of control apply to both teaching and learning. As Dewey suggests, education is fundamentally an interactive or transactional process. The challenges and confusion surrounding control issues address the normative role and responsibility afforded the teacher. It is the teacher who has the legitimate responsibility to define the curriculum and design the educational activities. Unfortunately, in traditional educational contexts there is little opportunity for collaboration in the planning process. That is, the student has little input or influence in the initial planning process or in defining expected outcomes of the educational experience. This creates the contradictory situation where the student is expected to assume responsibility for activities and an outcome over which they have had no input and offered little control. This is an issue that must be addressed considering "that a student's perceived control over his or her academic performance is strongly predictive of academic achievement" (Yeh, 2009, p. 229). Control reinforces effort and engagement.

The solution inherent to the transactional perspective is to give students opportunities for dialogue regarding outcome expectations, learning activities, and means of assessment. While some aspects of the educational transaction may not be open for negotiation, it is important that students share in this understanding. By being included in the larger process, and being provided choice where appropriate, students are given a sense of control and, therefore, are able to take responsibility for the quality of the educational outcome. It is collaborative efforts that help students assume responsibility for their learning.

The transactional perspective on teaching and learning reflects a dynamic balance of responsibility and control issues congruent with the educational purpose and the capabilities of the students. The flexibility and freedom of e-learning draws attention to fundamental responsibility and control issues. More work is needed before we can fully understand the implications that this technology can have on educational transactions.

THEORETICAL CONCEPTS

The key to understanding educational practices is to work back from the desired learning outcomes. In higher education, these outcomes are invariably associated with higher-order learning—becoming a critical and creative thinker. More recently, dispositions and abilities such as self-directedness and metacognition have been added, because it is not a simple matter of having students take responsibility for their learning. These dispositions and abilities must be developed for students if they are to assume increasing responsibility for their learning as required in a knowledge and creative society and economy.

The impermanence of public knowledge, along with the personal challenge of accommodating new ideas, necessitates an ability to think critically and be self-directed in monitoring and managing learning. Critical reflection and discourse are also demanded of the teacher for purposes of selecting and organizing content and for diagnosing possible misconceptions. Critical thinking is a holistic activity incorporating both reflective and shared activities. Furthermore, Lipman (2003) states, "the pedagogy of the 'community of inquiry' should be the methodology for the teaching of critical thinking . . ." (p. 3). Critical thinking and discourse is central to the Community of Inquiry theoretical framework.

Critical thinking and discourse are inseparable and reciprocal. As central as critical thinking and discourse is to higher education, empirical evidence of critical discourse precipitating critical thinking in e-learning environments has been difficult to find (Rourke & Kanuka, 2007). For this reason it is important to have a sense of what is meant by critical discourse. Discourse is more than casual conversation and is the external manifestation of higher-order learning. It is central to the ideal of the process of higher education. However, discourse is a complex and multidimensional process. Burbules (1993) points this out by describing four types of dialogue (i.e., discourse) for different orientations and purposes. The four types are—conversation, inquiry, debate and instruction. These dialogues overlap and can be combined in an educational experience. As Burbules (1993) states, "a degree of flexibility and pluralism in dialogical approach is essential" (p. 129). There is a place and need at various times in a community of inquiry for each type of dialogue or discourse. For example, dialogue for conversation (feeling of trust, respect, and concern) is directly associated with the need to create social presence. On the other hand, dialogue for inquiry and debate speaks to cognitive presence and the exploratory and confirmatory aspects of the Practical Inquiry model (see Chapter 5). Finally, dialogue as instruction clearly goes to the teaching presence element of the Community of Inquiry theoretical framework central to this book. The challenge, as we shall see in subsequent chapters, is how we design and deliver educational experiences in an e-learning environment that fully realize the potential for asynchronous discourse and functionally integrate its various forms.

Critical thinking is a model that naturally starts from the inside and looks out. This model reflects the various phases of critical thinking that iterate between the private and shared worlds of the individual. The phases of critical thinking (practical inquiry) are the triggering event, exploration, integration and resolution. For the individual to navigate through these phases of inquiry requires metacognitive awareness. On the other hand, self-directed learning is a complementary social model that takes an outside perspective and looks in. Self-directed learning addresses issues of monitoring understanding, management tasks and sustaining motivation. Self-directed learning and metacognitive awareness are two sides of the cognitive presence coin. Metacognition and self-direction pararallel critical thinking and discourse in a community of inquiry. They are emerging as important concepts toward understanding issues raised by technology and that have the potential to transfer enormous responsibility and control to the learner.

The concepts of metacognition and self-directed learning provide the theoretical mechanism for designing and implementing meaningful and worthwhile educational practice. That is, they describe the processes by which higher-order learning occurs. The next conceptual level in describing higher-order learning is to address approaches.

Approaches

The most promising research and knowledge base for understanding the educational experience outlines the conditions that would facilitate deep levels of understanding, not simply the recall of factual information. This work was pioneered by Marton (1988; Marton & Saljo, 1976) and confirmed by Entwistle (Entwistle & Ramsden, 1983) among others (Biggs, 1987). In its simplest form, this research described two distinct levels of information processing or understanding: surface-level processing, where the student has a reproductive or rote conception of learning and a corresponding learning strategy; and deep-level processing, where the intention is to comprehend and order the significance of the information as well as integrate it with existing knowledge.

It is clear that these approaches to learning and intentions are greatly influenced by the educational environment. That is, students adapt to the expectations and characteristics of the context under the immediate influence of the educator. The mechanism is that context strongly influences students' perceptions of learning tasks and, therefore, the strategies they adopt in approaching learning (Ramsden, 2003). A deep or surface approach to learning is a rational adaptation to contextual demands on the part of the student in order to ensure a successful outcome. Ramsden (1988) argues that there are three domains that influence perception and subsequent approaches to learning: assessment, curriculum, and teaching. There is, of course, considerable overlap among the domains.

Assessment (i.e., testing and grading) has a subtle but pervasive influence in shaping intentions and how students approach an educational experience. In fact, it may well be the most "critical situational influence on learning strategies" (Ramsden, 1988, p. 164). How students are assessed sends a very strong signal as to what is important and how they should approach learning. If the examination system is information recall, then students will, rationally, prepare for "recall of factual information to the detriment of a deeper level of understanding" (Marton & Saljo, 1976, p. 125). Obviously, the overwhelming concern of the vast majority of students is to pass. This in turn shapes how students approach learning and, thus, what they will learn. Therefore, assessment must be congruent with intended learning outcomes.

The second domain is associated with curriculum; in particular, workload, or the quantity of material to be assimilated in a defined period of time. Regardless of the student's inherent preference or intelligence, excessive curriculum demands dictate a surface approach to learning. A recent perspective on content coverage in collaborative environments suggests that "there is mounting evidence that less is more" (Lombardi, 2008, p. 4). It is not hard to see the influence and negative impact on deep approaches to learning of excessive content expectations beyond the control of the student. The challenge facing students and teachers is that "the world of knowledge is overwhelming, a vast ocean, horizonless, plunging to impossible depths" (Achenbach, 1999, p. A23). While pedagogy is essential in resolving this challenge, e-learning is an essential tool in creating an environment congruent with deep and meaningful approaches to learning.

The third domain, teaching presence, directly addresses this challenge by significantly influencing the approach to learning. The teacher has the greatest influence in shaping the learning environment and learning outcomes. To a large extent teachers define goals, content, and assessment. With the proliferation of information and the convenience of access to this information, it is the primary responsibility of the teacher to chart a way through this chaos, provide order, and create the conditions to encourage a deep approach to learning. From the student's perspective, this requires higher-order cognitive processing that includes critical and creative thinking.

The transactional perspective for effective teaching means moving beyond simple presentation methods. The transmission or presentational approach to teaching is highly prescriptive and is exemplified by the large lecture;

or in traditional distance education, a mass-produced study package. The presentational approach is inherently a one-way transmission of information, be it by lecture or independent study materials. Effective presentation depends on organization, clarity, and enthusiasm. While these are worthwhile teaching characteristics, they have not been shown to be sufficient in and of themselves to encourage or support deep approaches to learning.

As suggested in the phrase itself, the missing element in a presentational approach is interaction and critical discourse that is central to the transactional perspective. A transactional approach to teaching is based on the ideal of a community of learners and an educational process congruent with higher-order learning activities and outcomes. A transactional approach may include presentation characteristics, but these are balanced with flexibility, a supportive climate, and critical discourse. The transactional nature of a collaborative constructivist approach allows student participation in setting goals, selecting content and methods of assessment. This demands considerable professional judgment, especially with the freedom and autonomy provided by e-learning.

Principles

Coping with this complexity and the adoption of new technologies necessitates that teachers have a set of guiding principles. Previously, we identified the elements in this quest for quality learning outcomes to include assessment, workload and choice. The following principles reflect a transactional perspective and deep approach to learning. In essence, these principles are intended to create a supportive critical community of inquiry that is core to the e-learning framework described here. We define an educational community of inquiry as a group of individuals who collaboratively engage in purposeful critical discourse and reflection to construct personal meaning and confirm mutual understanding. In this regard, the CoI theoretical framework represents the process of creating a deep and meaningful (collaborative constructivist) learning experience through the development of three interdependent elements—social, cognitive and teaching presence.

The principles foreshadow the Community of Inquiry framework and are organized around the sub-elements of teaching presence (design, facilitation and direction); each of these in turn reflects the issues of social and cognitive presence.

The seven principles are:

1 Plan for the creation of open communication and trust.
2 Plan for critical reflection and discourse.
3 Establish community and cohesion.
4 Establish inquiry dynamics (purposeful inquiry).
5 Sustain respect and responsibility.

6 Sustain inquiry that moves to resolution.
7 Ensure assessment is congruent with intended processes and outcomes.

Success in creating an educational community of inquiry requires preparation, sustained presence and considerable pedagogic and content expertise. As we shall see, nothing less than this kind of teaching presence will ensure the full participation of students and deep approaches to learning, regardless of whether communication is face to face or mediated. However, in an e-learning context, there are exogenous technical variables that also must be considered in concert with these principles if we are to create and sustain a community of inquiry. Particular communications technologies must be understood as they directly and indirectly provide practical constraints in terms of the possibilities to create and sustain a community of inquiry.

TEXT-BASED COMMUNICATION

It is only in recent decades that linguists and members of other disciplines dealing with language regarded speech as clearly the primary form of human language. Writing was seen as the direct transfer of the information conveyed by speech into a visible medium. This equivalency assumption is beginning to be considered more closely, particularly within the body of literature on the use of text-based, computer-mediated communication for educational purposes (Feenberg, 1999; Garrison, 1997a; Garrison, Anderson, & Archer, 2000; Peters, 2000).

We argue that the differences in nature between spoken and written communication are, in fact, a key to understanding the effective use of computer-mediated communication and, specifically, e-learning and communities of inquiry (Archer, Garrison, & Anderson, 1999). While e-learning is a powerful communications tool, serious questions have been raised concerning the extent and degree to which text-based communication alters the "flow and structure" of higher-order teaching and learning, as compared to the more familiar environment of speech-based communication.

A full discussion of the characteristics of text-based communication will not be attempted here; however, we note that there is sufficient evidence to suggest that writing has some inherent and demonstrable advantages over speech when engaged in critical discourse and reflection. One obvious advantage is the permanent record afforded teachers and researchers. This, of course, contrasts with the ephemeral nature of discussions in face-to-face classroom environments. Furthermore, face-to-face conversation is generally less systematic, more exploratory, and less attentive to others' views.

Writing has long been used as both a process and product of rigorous critical thinking. The written word serves best to mediate recall and reflection, while the spoken word functions most effectively to mediate action (Wells, 1999). Ong (1982) argues that speech is a context into which all humans are born, and that speech is critical to the development of individual consciousness; however, "writing intensifies the sense of self and fosters more conscious interaction between persons" (p. 179). The characteristics of written, as compared to spoken, language would appear to affect the value of the former in facilitating higher-order learning through text-based media such as e-learning.

The apparent advantage of the written word in higher-order learning is supported in a study of questioning and cognitive functioning. It was found "that interaction in this on-line context was more intellectually demanding than that found in face-to-face" (Blanchette, 2001, p. 48). That is, the questions and responses were at a higher cognitive level than in a face-to-face verbal context. A possible (and probable) explanation is the asynchronous nature of written communication. It would appear that because students have more time to reflect, to be more explicit and to order content and issues, teachers were able to conduct high-level questioning. Finally, in an online context, administrative questions and issues were separated from academic discourse. That is, students could focus and reflect on higher-order cognitive questions and their responses.

Text-based communication has always been the preferred means of storing and sharing knowledge. This form of communication is central to e-learning and its use can only strengthen the educational experience through sustained online discourse and reflection. In short, text-based communication has considerable potential to facilitate critical discourse and reflection. There is every reason to believe that text-based communication in an e-learning context would have advantages to support collaborative constructivist approaches to learning. The importance of text-based communication will reassert itself in higher education through e-learning and as a result enhance the educational experience. However, better to understand the nature of text-based communication for educational purposes, we must explore more deeply the environment of a community of learners.

CONCLUSION

The information age and a networked world have forced educators to rethink the educational experience. It has become very clear that the value-add in a knowledge- and creative-based society will be a learning environment that develops and encourages the ability to think and learn both independently and collaboratively. Expectations for higher education are rising, and the foundational elements required for realizing these higher-order learning experiences have been outlined. This does not represent a reinvention of the educational transaction. But it does call for a refocusing and rededication to traditional higher education ideals. These ideals can be brought back within our grasp by technological developments.

Educators are particularly challenged when technologies such as e-learning are inserted into the equation. The reality is that "digital technologies [e-learning] require radically new and different notions of pedagogy" (Privateer, 1999, p. 70). In this regard, e-learning has considerable potential to alter the nature of the teaching and learning transaction. In fact, it has caused us to face up to some of the current deficiencies of higher education (such as large lectures) while providing possible solutions or ways to mitigate these shortcomings. Seen as part of a pedagogical solution, e-learning becomes an opportunity to examine and realize the ideals of the educational transaction described previously. Whether we realize the full benefit of e-learning will depend on understanding the context in which it will be introduced.

E-learning is a disruptive technology that is currently influencing how learning is approached in higher education. Higher education will inevitably be forced to recognize the revolutionary nature of learning technologies, and e-learning will be at the forefront. The strong influence of technology will change our ideas and approaches to cognition and pedagogy. As Privateer (1999) states: "It makes little sense for academia to continue a tradition of learning significantly at odds with technologies that are currently altering how humans learn and interact with each other in new learning communities" (p. 77).

It is the potential of e-learning to support and sustain learning communities to which we must turn our attention. The challenge is to understand this emerging educational environment and how we create and sustain communities of inquiry that will facilitate development of higher-order learning. The transactional perspective of teaching and learning adopted here is embedded in a critical community of inquiry where both reflection and discourse are utilized to facilitate the construction of personally meaningful and socially valid knowledge. It is to the Community of Inquiry theoretical framework that we turn our attention next.

Chapter 3

Community of Inquiry

Realizing the potential of e-learning does not imply that traditional educational values and practices will be declared obsolete. In fact, because of e-learning's unique capabilities to support asynchronous, collaborative communication in a dynamic and adaptable educational context, we will see a resurgence of traditional educational ideals. Re-valuing the traditional ideal of a community of learners is at the heart of the e-learning transformation. The framework we describe here is based upon the premise (supported by research and experience) that a community of learners is an essential, core element of an educational experience when higher-order learning is the desired learning outcome. By higher-order learning, we mean higher-order thinking "that is conceptually rich, coherently organized, and persistently exploratory" (Lipman, 1991, p. 19). These descriptions are congruent with the ideals of a community of inquiry in higher education.

The demands of an evolving knowledge society create expectations for individuals to be independent thinkers and, at the same time, interdependent, collaborative learners. These are the very core values and conditions of a worthwhile educational experience. The creation of knowledge in an educational context is a reflective and collaborative process made possible by a community of learners. The idealized view of education as a critical community of learners is no longer just an ideal, but has become a practical necessity in a society increasingly based on creativity and knowledge construction. It is within such a community of learners that the potential of e-learning can be fully realized.

The technology of e-learning has the capability both to precipitate private reflection and to precipitate public discourse. Its power is in its capability to connect people in personal and public ways. This unprecedented capability is fundamentally changing approaches to teaching and learning. However, along with this technological capability is the needed wisdom to create purposeful yet creative learning experiences with a balance between reflection and discourse. This balance is found through the teaching and learning transaction within the ethos of an open and critical community of inquiry.

THE LEARNING COMMUNITY

From both theoretical and empirical perspectives, the desirability and effectiveness of collaboration in achieving higher-order learning outcomes is seldom questioned. An increasingly prevalent and accepted position, made more practicable by e-learning, is that "the teaching of high-level concepts inevitably involves a considerable amount of discourse" (Bereiter, 1992, p. 352). Research in face-to-face and mediated educational contexts confirms the benefits of collaborative learning in supporting higher-order learning (Cecez-Kecmanovic & Webb 2000; Garrison & Archer, 2000; Johnson & Johnson, 2009). With the advances in e-learning technologies and the adoption of collaborative approaches to learning in higher education, we have gained a deeper understanding of collaborative learning processes.

A critical community of learners, from an educational perspective, is composed of teachers and students interacting with the specific purposes of facilitating, constructing, and validating understanding, and of developing capabilities that will lead to further learning. Such a community encourages cognitive independence and social interdependence simultaneously. It is the juxtaposition of both aspects of this seemingly contradictory relationship that creates the spark that ignites a true educational experience that has personal value and socially redeeming outcomes. In many respects, education is a purposeful and guided activity in which the individual is making sense of societal knowledge and educational experiences. The learning community is a fusion of individual (subjective) and shared (objective) worlds.

E-learning from a formal educational perspective must be appreciated in terms of the nature of the transaction between and among teacher and students. It is a serious mistake to categorize teaching and learning in terms of extreme positions. E-learning is no more inherently learner-centered than traditional face-to-face learning is inherently teacher-centered. Like any educational experience, successful e-learning depends on the ability of the educator to create learning environments that motivate students and facilitate meaningful and worthwhile learning activities. It serves no useful purpose to use labels to artificially polarize teacher and student roles and responsibilities. Roles change and the balance of control shifts throughout a formal educational experience.

However, before describing the conceptual framework for a community of inquiry, we will briefly turn our attention to the origins of e-learning— computer conferencing. Early in the development of computer conferencing, it became apparent that it was not an exact replication of the conventional face-to-face classroom experience. As a result, largely because of the asynchronous and text-based nature of this communication, many investigators realized that computer conferencing represented a qualitatively different approach to learning (Harasim, 1987; Kaye, 1987). The point is that e-learning has its roots in computer conferencing (Cleveland-Innes & Garrison,

2010) and not traditional distance education. As such, e-learning should not be seen as synonymous with distance education. Historically, distance education was purposed to bridge geographical distances and was embedded in the industrial model and institutions focused on cost-effective access. The ability of e-learning to support a collaborative learning experience very much challenged the dominant world-view of distance education as being a largely independent, self-instructional approach to learning. In addition, "most e-learning in American higher education is not used for distance teaching purposes" (Guri-Rosenblit, 2009, p. 94). Therefore, while there is overlap with distance education, e-learning must be considered a distinct branch of the educational evolutionary tree.

The affordability and ubiquity of e-learning technologies make it a disruptive technology in higher education. The challenge is to use e-learning in ways that support new and more effective approaches to learning. Communications technologies, such as e-learning, "will reveal new approaches to the teaching and learning transaction that can enhance the quality of learning outcomes in higher education by increasing access to critical communities of learners, not simply access to information" (Garrison & Anderson, 1999, p. 51). While higher education is not exempt from accessibility demands, we must be clear as to what students should be accessing. The best place to start thinking about e-learning is in its ability to support high levels of interactivity. E-learning, properly designed, has all the potential to revitalize the traditions of higher education without sacrificing its values.

A THEORETICAL FRAMEWORK

We have previously alluded to the importance of context and specifically argued for the creation of a community of learners to facilitate critical discourse and reflection. Individual knowledge construction is very much shaped by the social environment. That is, an environment with choice and a diversity of perspectives will encourage critical and creative inquiry. Such a community of inquiry is a requisite for higher-order learning and the core element in the e-learning framework described here.

Lipman (2003) argues for the necessity of a community of inquiry for the operationalization of critical or reflective thinking and as an educational methodology. This is a teacher-guided, non-authoritarian community where societal knowledge is revealed in an equivocal, multidisciplinary manner whose goal is to structure relationships (order) to achieve understanding and develop "rationality tempered by judgment" (Lipman, 2003, p. 11). Citing Dewey, Lipman (2003) notes that the great mistake of mainstream education was "to neglect the process and fixate upon the product" (p. 20). A community of inquiry is crucial in precipitating and maintaining reflection and discourse (inquiry) and the development of judgment in constructing and testing meaning (product). In short, inquiry is the active search for meaning. With the collaboration of the group, the individual assumes responsibility to construct meaning and make sense of the educational experience.

In a community of inquiry there is both rationality and freedom. As Lipman (2003, p. 20) states, a community of inquiry is where

> . . . students listen to one another with respect, build on one another's ideas, challenge one another to supply reasons for otherwise unsupported opinions, assist each other in drawing inferences from what has been said, and seek to identify one another's assumptions. A community of inquiry attempts to follow the inquiry where it leads rather than being penned in by the boundary lines of existing disciplines.

In other words, a community of inquiry provides the environment in which students can take responsibility and control of their learning through negotiating meaning, diagnosing misconceptions, and challenging accepted beliefs—essential ingredients for deep and meaningful learning outcomes. As Schrage (1989, p. 5) notes:

> Creating a shared understanding is simply a different task than exchanging information. It's the difference between being deeply involved in a conversation and lecturing to a group. The words are different, the tone is different, the attitude is different, and the tools are different.

Most importantly here, the evidence supports the position that collaborative inquiry can be supported in an e-learning context (Garrison & Arbaugh, 2007). Research supports the positive relationship between perceived learning and a sense of community (Liu, Magjuka, Bonk & Lee, 2007; Rovai, 2002). One study demonstrated that a stronger sense of community (more peer interactions) would lead to increased learning (higher grades) in asynchronous environments (Harvey, Moller, Huett, Godshalk & Downs, 2007). In fact, considering the reflective and explicit nature of the communication, as well as the opportunity to access data sources, it is argued that there are distinct advantages to creating a community of inquiry in an e-learning environment. The permanence of text-based communication lends itself to reflection and the ability to challenge assumptions as well as edit text and rewrite positions.

We have identified in various forms, although not explicitly, the three key elements or presences that must be considered when planning and delivering an e-learning experience. The Community of Inquiry (CoI) theoretical framework represents a process of creating a deep and meaningful (collaborative constructivist) learning experience through the development of three interdependent elements—social presence, cognitive presence and teaching presence. A presence is a sense of being or identity created through

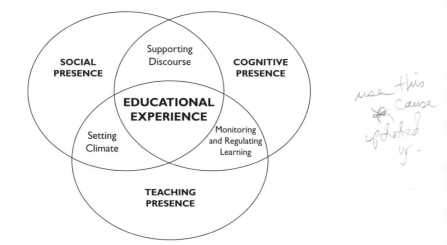

Figure 3.1 Community of Inquiry

interpersonal communication. A brief outline of each is given here. The implications of the interdependent elements in ensuring a collaborative constructivist e-learning educational experience are fully explored in later chapters. Figure 3.1 shows the relationship of the three elements.

Social Presence

Social presence is the ability of participants to identify with a group, communicate purposefully in a trusting environment, and develop personal and affective relationships progressively by way of projecting their individual personalities (Garrison, 2009b). However, when the medium is the written word, establishing social presence can be challenging. Due to the lack of non-verbal communication, the shift from spoken communication to the written communication of an e-learning context presents a special challenge for establishing social presence. Written communication lacks a sense of immediacy described here as communication (verbal and written) that builds interpersonal relationships. Immediacy is important to a supportive and secure learning environment because it reduces personal risk and increases acceptance, particularly during critical discourse that questions ideas and understanding.

Not only is teaching higher-order cognitive skills more successful when co-operatively based (Resnick, 1987), cognitive presence is also enhanced and sustained when social presence is established (Akyol & Garrison, in press; Fabro & Garrison 1998; Gunawardena, 1995; Liu, Gomez & Yen, 2009). Socio-emotional communication in text-based communication is possible through the use of compensating strategies, such as the adaptation of textual behaviors to reveal social and relational messages (Walther, 1992). Compensating redundancies benefit all communication that carries the potential for misunderstanding. Attention must be given to establishing and sustaining appropriate social presence if the full potential of e-learning is to be realized.

Cognitive Presence

At its core, education is about learning, but a specific kind of social learning defined by process and outcome. To this end, cognitive presence speaks to intent, process, and learning outcomes. We see cognitive presence "as the extent to which learners are able to construct and confirm meaning through sustained reflection and discourse in a critical community of inquiry" (Garrison, Anderson & Archer, 2001, p. 11). Reflection is consistent with the ability to think critically (rational judgment) (see Chapter 6) while discourse relies on trust, communicative relationships, and communication purposefully focused toward understanding a dilemma or problem. As we shall see, they are inseparable in practice. In essence, cognitive presence is a condition of higher-order thinking and learning.

Cognitive presence is described in the context of a general model of critical thinking. The primary source for this model is Garrison & Archer (2000) but this is largely derivative of Dewey's (1933) works on reflective thinking. The practical inquiry model, discussed in Chapter 6, is the starting-point for understanding and operationalizing cognitive presence. This model represents a generic structure of critical inquiry that is consistent with the complementarity of reflection and discourse and the multi-phased educational process designed to construct meaning (emphasis on reflection) and confirm understanding (emphasis on discourse).

Teaching Presence

The third mutually reinforcing element in a community of inquiry is teacher presence. One of the difficulties with early computer conferencing was sustaining participation and high levels of discourse (Gunawardena, 1991; Hiltz & Turoff, 1993). Low levels of interest and participation were rooted in a lack of structure and focus resulting from an excessively "democratic" approach. While there must be full and open participation, for a purposeful educational experience there is an inherent need for an architect and leader to design, facilitate, and inform the transaction.

Therefore, teaching presence is defined as "the design, facilitation and direction of cognitive and social processes for the purpose of realizing personally meaningful and educationally worthwhile learning outcomes" (Anderson, Rourke, Garrison & Archer, 2001). As can be deduced from this definition, teaching presence brings all the elements of a community of inquiry together in a balanced and functional relationship congruent with the intended outcomes and the needs and capabilities of the learners. This, of course, is an enormously imposing task under the best of circumstances. Teaching presence represents perhaps a greater challenge in an e-learning environment.

Indicators

For theoretical and practical purposes, a template has been constructed consisting of categories of indicators within each of the three core elements that reflect meaningful learning activities commonly found in an e-learning environment. Indicators are key words or phrases that suggest the presence of the three elements and, in total, a quality educational experience. Table 3.1 provides the template that guides our assessment of the nature and quality of an e-learning experience. This has been useful to code transcripts in the early stages of this research and thereby gauge specifically what is occurring within an e-learning community of inquiry. This template has lead to the construction of a quantitative survey instrument (see below and Appendix).

The categories for cognitive, social, and teaching presence emerged from the literature and were refined within the Community of Inquiry conceptual framework. Social presence is structured according to affective communication, open communication, and group cohesion (see Chapter 5 for modifications with regard to affective communication). Considerable thought and discussion, based on an exploratory study of computer conferencing transcripts, resulted in the three first-order categories. The cognitive presence categories correspond to each of the practical inquiry phases. A similar

Table 3.1 Community of Inquiry Categories and Indicators

Elements	Categories	Indicators (examples only)
Social presence	Personal/affective	Self projection/expressing emotions
	Open communication	Learning climate/risk-free expression
	Group cohesion	Group identity/collaboration
Cognitive presence	Triggering event	Sense of puzzlement
	Exploration	Information exchange
	Integration	Connecting ideas
	Resolution	Applying new ideas
Teaching presence	Design and organization	Setting curriculum and methods
	Facilitating discourse	Shaping constructive exchange
	Direct instruction	Focusing and resolving issues

methodology resulted in the emergence of three teaching-presence categories: design and organization, building understanding, and direct instruction. Examples of indicators for all the categories and elements were initially theoretically derived, however, their validity has been tested and the results are discussed in subsequent chapters.

THEORETICAL DEVELOPMENT

The Community of Inquiry (CoI) framework was first described in a publication over a decade ago (Garrison, Anderson & Archer, 2000). The original framework was based upon a review of the higher education teaching and learning literature, a few initial studies, and the experiences of the research team. It has not only held up remarkably well but has been referenced in hundreds of publications. Studies have consistently demonstrated the stability of the CoI framework through large, cross-institutional studies (Arbaugh, Cleveland-Innes, Diaz, Garrison, Ice, Richardson, Shea & Swan, 2008).

These findings have created the conditions to construct a quantitative CoI survey instrument that has greatly expanded research interest in this theoretical framework (Arbaugh et al., 2008). The results of this study provided an instrument that is a valid, reliable, and efficient measure of the CoI framework (see Appendix). Research using this instrument has confirmed the CoI structure and provided new insights and questions. This instrument has opened up the study of e-learning in general and the CoI framework specifically to a wide range of research. This instrument can be particularly useful in conducting large-scale multi-institutional studies. One recent study concluded ". . . that a three factor solution emerged regardless of the underlying socio-epistemological orientation" (Akyol, Ice, Garrison & Mitchell, 2010, p. 67); and another study that included both course rating and importance rating concluded, "factor analysis of multiplicative scores [course and importance ratings] . . . supported the CoI model's tripartite structure" (Diaz, Swan, Ice & Kupczynski, 2010, p. 22).

It is important to appreciate that each individual in the collaborative constructivist educational experience manifests each of the presences. All participants assume aspects of each of the presences. The exact nature and the degree to which they reflect each of the presences will depend on the individual and the task at hand. Most often this balance shifts as the educational experience progresses (students assume increased teaching presence). However, it should be kept in mind that there is no "learner" presence or "teacher" presence per se. Each participant (teacher and students) assumes varying aspects and degrees of teaching presence (admittedly the instructor will generally exhibit greater teaching presence). For example, the goal is always to have students assume more teaching presence and become increasingly self-directed. Individually and collaboratively, students will assume increasing cognitive and metacognitive responsibility as they become more competent and confident. In addition, students will likely learn to facilitate discourse as social presence grows through trust, communication, and cohesion.

Another important step forward in CoI research was the focus on the dynamic relationships among the presences. Understanding the dynamics of a community of inquiry helps to understand the community as a whole and the validity of the framework itself. While the CoI framework was intended to describe the interdependent nature of the presences, much of the early work was focused on defining and exploring the individual presences. The individual learning experience is a function of the shared relationships among social, cognitive, and teaching presence. In this regard, it has been shown that students report significantly higher perceived learning and satisfaction and "that the collaborative learning model should be the foundation upon which online courses are designed and delivered" (Arbaugh & Benbunan-Fich, 2006, p. 435).

In collaborative learning environments it is contradictory to talk about teacher and learner presence as if these were independent responsibilities and activities. This may be a hold-over from passive conventional higher education or traditional distance education enterprises where the independence of the learner is necessitated by access barriers. However, as we have argued here, the core e-learning capability is sustained communication and collaboration regardless of physical separation or time shifting.

A THEORY?

The research on the CoI framework has raised the question of whether it should be elevated to that of a theory. The CoI framework represents a coherent set of articulated elements and models describing a higher educational learning experience. However, to constitute a comprehensive theory there must be other features present. Dubin (1978) suggests that in addition to units or elements there must be defined relationships (laws of interaction), boundaries that limit its relevance, and system states (how elements act differently in their relations). Once these basic features are in place, then propositions, empirical indicators, and hypotheses can be derived. A theory is essential for interpreting the findings of empirical research and the possible refinement of the theory. We argue here that these basic features of a theory are in place in the CoI framework. Moreover, the CoI framework has been shown that it has the ability to generate hypotheses and provide the theoretical context to interpret findings. It is, therefore, argued that it should at least be considered a nascent theory of e-learning.

When the CoI framework was first proposed, the aspect that was lacking, to be considered a complete theory, was the detail and completeness of explanation to understand the nature of the relationships among the elements and the development of the system as a whole to rigorously define the relationships and describe system states. In interpreting the data from the research over this last decade (to be discussed in subsequent chapters) it is clear that it has provided a parsimonious structure and understanding of a complex phenomenon. The number of research studies using the CoI framework clearly indicates that researchers were able to make propositions (predictions), generate hypotheses, and empirically test these hypotheses. A decade of research has provided empirical findings to describe the nature of the interactions among the elements as well as the dynamic balance of the CoI system over time. To this point, it has been stated that there "is growing evidence that the CoI framework does account for much of the complexity of the teaching and learning transaction" (Garrison & Arbaugh, 2007, p. 166).

One final feature that needs further discussion is its boundary or area of application. The reason for mentioning this is that the CoI framework was first proposed to provide some order to the complexities of studying and understanding computer conferencing and online learning. It has since been used to study blended learning (Garrison & Vaughan, 2008) and with this its implicit boundary has been expanded to all of e-learning as we have defined it here. However, it was noted at its inception that it was a generic model generated from the literature and experiences of the authors in higher education generally (Garrison, Anderson & Archer, 2000). The point is that the CoI framework could well be applied to face-to face higher education (Archer, 2010), although the only known application beyond purely online learning is in a blended learning context. One other point with regard to boundaries is the perception of factors such as discipline, student characteristics, and technology that were considered exogenous variables in the original description. While these are worthy of study in terms of their relationship to the elements of the CoI, they continue to be considered indirect variables for reasons of parsimony.

Considering the previous discussion and the theoretical state of the CoI, we propose that the CoI framework has moved rapidly in the direction of a comprehensive theory and is consistent with the features of a theory. Its adequacy as a theory will be based on its coherence and explanatory power (i.e., logic) (Dubin, 1978) and the CoI framework would appear to have sufficient coherence and explanatory power to be considered a theory. Moreover, its usefulness will be judged by its adoption and the consensus of researchers. To date, in terms of its citation and use to frame studies, the evidence would suggest it constitutes a theory. As a theory, the CoI provides the means to study and understand the relationships among the elements and learning in a collaborative educational environment. Therefore, we argue that the CoI meets the primary goal of a theory (Dubin, 1978).

To be clear, much work remains to detail the explanatory power and completeness of the CoI theory. However, it would seem that the CoI is closer to a comprehensive theory than it is to a framework. For this reason, in the remainder of this second edition we shift from the terminology of the CoI framework to the CoI theoretical framework. At the same time, it is clear that judgments of what constitutes a theory are based on complex arguments; so, consistent with all scientific endeavors, in the final analysis it will be left to others to judge whether the CoI has reached, or how it might reach, the threshold of theory.

CONCLUSION

This chapter has outlined the concepts and elements that we believe will provide the order and insight into understanding the complexities and potential of an e-learning experience. Within the conceptual framework of a learning community, the Community of Inquiry framework was developed. The framework and its constituent parts have guided the theoretical and empirical investigation described in this book. We believe it is the most coherent theory to date in guiding the research and practice of e-learning and that it has enormous potential to design, guide, and assess e-learning approaches, strategies, and techniques.

Chapter 4

Social Presence

The early adopters of e-learning immediately recognized its potential to support a collaborative learning experience. Along with this, however, came the need to create a welcoming learning environment that would serve the educational needs for which it was intended. This precipitated considerable thought and discussion with regard to replicating a classroom experience. What was not fully appreciated was that creating a community of learners through an asynchronous text-based means of communication represented a qualitative shift from that of a real-time, verbal, face-to-face mode of communication. As such, the challenge of creating an open and cohesive community of inquiry in a medium that provides no visual cues other than words or images on a screen presented a unique challenge for educators.

To create the type of community that will support higher learning requires an understanding of the nature of social interaction in a non-verbal environment. A cohesive community can be created based upon establishing friendships or it can be based upon other common purposes such as specific educational goals. A community will sustain itself based upon how well individuals and the group achieve their goals. However, achieving educational goals in a collaborative environment must also consider the socio-emotional issues of the participants. Cohesion and a sense of belonging are essential attributes in a community of inquiry.

A NON-VERBAL COMMUNITY

Community is integral to all aspects of life. Community represents the fusion of the individual and the group; the psychological and sociological; the reflective and the collaborative. This is no less so in terms of creating and sustaining a community of learners. The implicit denial of community has been the greatest shortcoming of traditional distance education with its focus on prescriptive course packages to be assimilated by the student in isolation. This is based upon an assumption that learning is an individual experience and that there is little need to negotiate meaning and confirm understanding. However, education is a collaborative experience, which includes a sense of belonging and acceptance in a group with common interests. As such, we must reflect upon what social presence means in an e-learning community that is distinguished by the written word as the predominant mode of communication.

The original working definition of social presence was "the ability of participants in a community of inquiry to project themselves socially and emotionally, as 'real' people (i.e., their full personality), through the medium of communication being used" (Garrison, Anderson & Archer, 2000, p. 94). The premise was that it is inconceivable to think that one could create a community without some degree of social presence. The challenge, however, was to understand the nature of social presence in a purposeful community focused on academic inquiry that involves sustained critical discourse (i.e., cognitive presence). The point is that social presence must support inquiry and the achievement of specific learning outcomes. So the question became, "Why is social presence important and what does it look like?"

Asynchronous text-based communication would appear to present a special challenge in creating a social environment and community of inquiry. Communication theorists have drawn considerable attention to the lack of non-verbal communication cues that are considered to be crucial in forming collaborative relationships. Short, Williams & Christie (1976) concluded a review of media studies by stating that the "absence of the visual channel reduces the possibilities for expression of socio-emotional material and decreases the information available about the other's self-image, attitudes, moods, and reactions" (p. 59). The authors use the term social presence to argue that the medium of communication is a serious limiting factor to shared social presence. The question was whether this is fatal to forming and sustaining a fully collaborative community of inquiry? Does text-based communication provide the means to communicate socio-emotional content necessary for building a social community, of feeling connected, and preventing a feeling of anomie? On the other hand, can teachers and students acquire and use compensating communication skills for quality collaborative learning experiences?

Doubts were raised about the intimate connection of social presence to the characteristics of the medium (Kim, in press). Gunawardena (1995) was instrumental in redefining social presence in terms of whether participants are perceived as "being real" (Gunawardena & Zittle, 1997, p. 8). This was the beginning of important research into social presence and the catalyst for the CoI theoretical framework. The research question was whether the nature of written language can compensate for the lack of visual cues such as body language and verbal intonation which have a profound effect on how a message is interpreted in a face-to-face environment. Or, alternatively, might this medium exhibit other characteristics or properties that provide an advantage to the less extraverted student and, overall, offer the potential for greater equality and participation?

The simple answer to these complex questions is that it has been shown that students can and do overcome the lack of non-verbal communication by establishing familiarity through the use of greetings, encouragement, paralinguistic emphasis (e.g., capitals, punctuation, emoticons), and personal vignettes (i.e., self-disclosure) (Garrison & Arbaugh, 2007; Rourke & Anderson, 2002). The implicit understanding of the purpose of a community of inquiry carries with it social cues to help shape the academic nature of the interaction that is required. The fact that text-based communication is a relatively lean medium may not be a serious limitation. As we have argued, the characteristics of a text-based medium as being reflective, explicit, and precise may well have inherent advantages in focusing and elevating the academic level of the exchange. That is, written communication may well be more effective for facilitating critical thinking and discourse.

The conclusion is that the apparent limitations of text-based e-learning may well provide advantages not possible in a face-to-face educational context. The leanness or richness of the medium will be defined by the task at hand (i.e., purpose) and by the compensating opportunities the medium affords. With regard to the affordance of the medium, research conducted on text-based e-learning has consistently demonstrated a capacity for a high level of interpersonal communication resulting in perceived satisfaction and learning (Garrison & Arbaugh, 2007; Kim, in press).

It is argued here that social presence is an important mediating variable to collaboration and critical discourse. Establishing relationships and a sense of belonging are important. However, social presence does not mean supporting engagement for purely social purposes where students are not predisposed to be skeptical or critical of ideas expressed for fear that they might hurt somebody's feelings and damage a relationship. Social presence in an academic context means creating a climate that supports and encourages probing questions, skepticism and the contribution of explanatory ideas. Sustaining critical thinking and discourse requires a sense of belonging that must develop over time.

> What sustains a dialogue over time is not only lively inter-change about the topic at hand, but a certain commitment to one's partner; a commitment that might not precede the dialogue, but arises only gradually in the spirit of the engagement.
>
> (Burbules, 1993, p. 15)

A community of inquiry must be both inclusive and critical. It is through balancing these seemingly contradictory but complementary social and academic elements that a quality learning environment is created. This is where e-learning can be a very effective medium for supporting an intellectually challenging, yet respectful, community of inquiry.

DEVELOPMENTS

While social presence concerns have attracted great interest from the beginning of computer conferencing and online learning, the field is still in need of further research. Much of the work on social presence was on the social-emotional in isolation from a formal academic context. It was not until the development of social presence within the CoI theoretical framework that it moved from a largely affective construct to a more complex and dynamic element that included issues such as open communication and cohesion. This was in recognition of the purposeful academic nature of a community of inquiry. However, questions remain with regard to the affective dimension of social presence.

What precipitated the re-examination of the social presence construct presented here was the research by Rogers & Lea (2005). They found that when there is shared social identity with the group, group cohesion is enhanced and the group will be more productive. More specifically, social presence is enhanced when individuals identify with the group *and its purpose* as opposed to connecting with specific individual members. Put another way:

> Social presence was enabled through the emphasis on the shared social identity at the level of the collaborating group rather than the creation of interpersonal bonds between individual group members.
>
> (Rogers & Lea, 2005, p. 156)

If this is the case, emphasis early in a course of studies should focus on the social dimensions of open communication and cohesion that are best developed from a shared purpose and group identity. Climate and interpersonal relationships need to be given time to develop and not distract from the academic purpose of the course of studies.

Such a view of social presence is consistent with a formal educational environment where there are common goals and establishing a purposeful community of inquiry is appropriate. The primary reason students are there is to learn about a specific subject, not necessarily to develop personal relationships. The sense of group identity is then consistent with the other dimensions of social presence—open communication and group cohesion. Identification with the purpose of the group in an educational context has a stronger influence on academic behavior than individual relationships. That said, interpersonal relationships will develop and should be encouraged to the degree that they do not conflict with group identity and the core purpose of the community of inquiry.

This raises questions with regard to the nature of the social presence dimensions, in particular the affective dimension. Setting climate may be more about a feeling of belonging to the group and less about affectively connecting with others on a personal basis. The question is whether there should be so much focus on the interpersonal (personal identity) at the beginning of the course. Perhaps we need to re-examine the affective dimension from the perspective of group identity. Parenthetically, affective concerns were raised by Shea, Hayes, Vickers, Gozza-Cohen, Uzner, Mehta, Valchova & Rangan (2010) when they noted the difficulty of identifying indicators of affect and concluded that social presence is in need of additional specification. Considering that affect is associated with each of the dimensions of social presence and the inherent academic orientation of a community of inquiry, it has been suggested that perhaps the specification of the affect dimension should be revised (Garrison, 2009b).

In this regard, we offer a revised definition of social presence as the ability of participants to identify with the group or course of study, communicate purposefully in a trusting environment, and develop personal and affective relationships progressively by way of projecting their individual personalities (Garrison, 2009b). A significant advantage of this definition is that it better conveys the dynamic nature of the social presence construct in a progressively developing community of inquiry. That is, it places purpose and open communication within the community as a priority that then leads to increased group cohesion. Through engagement in collaborative activities students develop an academic climate and personal relationships grow naturally over time. In this way, personal relationships enhance and do not interfere with academic discourse and group identity (i.e., cohesion). Furthermore, the pattern of open communication (purposeful discourse) is set and personal sensitivities (i.e., a reluctance to criticize resulting from close relationships) are less likely to occur. As noted by Lea et al. (cited in Rogers & Lea, 2005), "environments rich in interpersonal information may, in fact, undermine group identity and result in process losses for the collaborating group" (p. 153).

The possibility that social presence might undermine cognitive presence was, in fact, demonstrated in a study by Jahng, Nielsen & Chan (2010) when they found that increased social communications reduced cognitive communications. They conclude that "there may be an appropriate level of social communication that supports collaborative activity more generally directed at a learning goal [cognitive presence]" (Jahng et al., 2010, p. 54). The bottom line is that excessive emphasis on developing interpersonal relationships may have deleterious effects on the academic functioning of the group if the individual bonds are stronger than the identity to the group and its goals. Therefore, excessive time on introductions may well be counterproductive. The implications from a practical perspective are that while individuals should be encouraged to provide personal bios, this must not distract from the academic activities of the group. In general, this suggests that members of the community should develop relationships naturally and progressively through the purposeful and collaborative inquiry process.

This discussion of the natural progression of interpersonal relationships raises the important issue of the dynamic of social presence. Theoretically, it was predicted that open communication indicators will be high at the beginning of a community of inquiry and will diminish slightly over time with experience and feedback as to the rules of engagement. It is hypothesized that both group cohesion and interpersonal indicators will likely increase and plateau. In support of this, it has been shown that open communication does decrease over time while cohesion increases (Akyol & Garrison, 2008). In addition, interpersonal communication creates camaraderie after a period of intense association (Brown, 2001). This speaks to the recommendation not to focus excessively on the affective and personal communication among participants.

At the same time, Shea et al. (2010) note that it is not clear as to the dynamics of the social presence dimensions. While theoretical predictions of the importance of social presence communication as a whole suggest a decline over time (Garrison & Arbaugh, 2007), fluctuations in social presence have been shown to be affected by teaching presence. Shea et al. (2010) state that "as instructor teaching presence rises or falls, there is a correlating rise or fall in student social presence" (p. 13). One interpretation of this is that this may be the result of the emphasis on social or cognitive presence by the instructor. In other words, a strong focus on the academic tasks may well see a fall in social presence indicators and, conversely, an instructor who models strong social presence will very likely raise the level of social presence in the community as a whole. The key, however, is that this modeling must complement the specific academic task.

Notwithstanding the considerable research into social presence, there is much to understand with regard to the construct itself and its relationship to the other presences. An important area of research that has helped us understand social presence is the empirical testing of the causal relationships among the three presences in a community of inquiry. Only a few years ago it was pointed out that few studies have examined the presences simultaneously (Garrison & Arbaugh, 2007). Recent studies have explored this issue and found that social presence plays a mediating role between teaching and cognitive presence (Garrison, Cleveland-Innes & Fung, 2010; Shea & Bidjerano, 2009a). Moreover, it was found that teaching presence is essential to establishing social presence. These relationships among the presences were explored more deeply in a study that looked at their progression over time (Akyol & Garrison, 2008). First, it was shown that each of the social presence categories developed at different rates. For example, it showed that affective expression dropped significantly while group cohesion increased significantly over time. This is consistent with a study by Vaughan & Garrison (2006) that also found a decrease in affective and open communication and an increase in group cohesion.

There have also been a number of studies exploring the relationship of social presence with satisfaction, learning outcomes, and retention. A review of this research found evidence of a relationship between social presence, satisfaction, and perceived learning (Garrison & Arbaugh, 2007; Kim, in press). Several recent studies confirmed previous findings that show a significant relationship between social presence and satisfaction (Akyol & Garrison, 2008; Akyol & Garrison, in press b). However, there is also a study that has shown a significant relationship between collaborative learning and satisfaction but not between social presence and overall satisfaction (So & Brush, 2008). The explanation is that social presence is a complex concept that is associated with both social and academic factors (reinforcing the interdependency of the presences). Participants in a community of inquiry may be distinguishing between social interaction and meaningful academic collaboration. Since communities of inquiry are task/goal oriented, participants may be satisfied with their connection to members of the community but not necessarily with the academic activities and feedback. An example of this is a study by Nippard & Murphy (2007) who found that expressions of social presence were of a digressive nature and often drew attention away from the delivery of the content.

Recent studies have also confirmed previous studies in that they have shown social presence to be associated with perceived learning (Caspi & Blau, 2008) and final grades (Akyol & Garrison, in press a; Kang & Kim, 2006; Liu, Gomez & Yen, 2009). Theoretically, it is argued that social presence that promotes group identity (cohesion) can create a greater sense of perceived and actual learning. Finally, although we could find only one study that looked at social presence and retention, there is one large-scale study that provides an interesting insight into re-enrolment in fully online programs (Boston, Diaz, Gibson, Ice, Richardson & Swan, 2009). This study has shown a significant relationship between social presence and retention that is consistent with previous research into social integration in higher education. The authors conclude, "Social interaction remains a crucial factor for student retention" (Boston et al., 2009, p. 77).

We have made considerable progress in understanding social presence and there is evidence of the multidimensional nature of this construct. Kim (in press) "confirmed the multidimensionality of social presence". Based upon an extensive review of the concept and factor analysis his four-factor solution includes the three dimensions of social presence as defined within the CoI theoretical framework. However, he suggests a fourth factor labeled as "mutual attention and support". The difficulty, as Kim suggests, is that this reflects learning support which would represent an overlap with teaching or cognitive presence. The items loading on this factor or dimension appear to reflect aspects of the learning process (cognitive presence) and its support (teaching presence). To reinforce the point made previously, it is important to study and understand the social presence construct in relation to the other presences and in the larger educational context.

Notwithstanding this, the conclusion is that social presence is a multidimensional construct in need of further study. Research is required better to understand the structure of the construct, patterns of development in concert with the other presences, and its influence on dependent variables such as learning outcomes and retention. The first step to achieving these goals is to outline clearly the dimensions of social presence.

CATEGORIES OF SOCIAL PRESENCE

The original classification scheme for social presence was constructed through an iterative process. This consisted of a theoretical analysis of the literature as well as the analysis and coding of computer conferencing transcripts. This resulted in three broad categories of social presence indicators consisting of affective communication, open communication, and cohesive communicative responses. However, sharing socio-emotional feelings in a purposeful community of inquiry should not be the primary focus of social presence. The view here is that this will occur and friendships will develop when a climate for open communication is created. In this regard, we suggest that the affective communication needs to be expanded and its importance qualified in terms of the other social presence categories. Consideration needs to be given to understanding the structure and dynamic nature of social presence by juxtaposing personal and group identification issues discussed previously.

Interpersonal Communication

After a decade of research into the CoI theoretical framework it would appear that affective responses may not be the defining characteristic of social presence. As argued previously, group identity takes precedence over personal identity. What is crucial at the outset of establishing a community of inquiry is interpersonal communication responsible for setting the academic climate for open and academically purposeful communication. Interest and persistence is essential to a learning experience that goes beyond simply attending to affective communication. Interpersonal communication creates a climate and sense of belonging to the group and its educational goals. It is an essential facilitating condition for engagement in meaningful discourse. A respectful and supportive climate reflects the initial conditions necessary for critical reflection and discourse.

There are three major indicators of interpersonal communication (see Table 4.1). First, when physical cues and vocal intonations are not present, expression of respect and welcome can be communicated through other means such as emoticons and capitalization. Second, beyond these more unconventional means of expressing feelings, language itself through the content of messages is a very powerful interpersonal communicator. Perhaps the easiest to appreciate but most difficult to code is related to humor references. Humor and personal references convey goodwill and suggest that

Table 4.1 Social Presence Classification and Indicators

Category	Indicators	Definition	Example
Interpersonal communication	Affective expression	Conventional expressions of emotion, or unconventional expressions of emotion, including repetitious punctuation, conspicuous capitalization, emoticons	"I just can't stand it when . . .!!!!" "ANYBODY OUT THERE!"
	Self-disclosure	Presents biographies, details of personal life outside of class, or expresses vulnerability	"Where I work, this is what we do . . ." "I just don't understand this question"
	Use of humor	Teasing, cajoling, irony, understatements, sarcasm	"The banana crop in Calgary is looking good this year ;-)"
Open communication	Continuing a thread	Using reply feature of software, rather than starting a new thread	Software dependent, e.g., "Subject: Re" or "Branch from"
	Quoting from others' messages	Using software features to quote others' entire messages, or cutting and pasting selections of others' messages	Software dependent, e.g., "Martha writes:" or text prefaced by less-than symbol <
	Referring explicitly to others' messages	Direct references to contents of others' posts	"In your message, you talked about Moore's distinction between . . ."
	Asking questions	Students ask questions of other students or the moderator	"Anyone else had experience with WEBCT?"
	Complimenting, expressing appreciation	Complimenting others or contents of others' messages	"I really like your interpretation of the reading"
	Expressing agreement	Expressing agreement with others or content of others' messages	"I was thinking the same thing. You really hit the nail on the head"
Cohesive communication	Vocatives	Addressing or referring to participants by name	"I think John made a good point." "John, what do you think?"
	Addresses or refers to the group using inclusive pronouns	Addresses the group as we, us, our, group	"Our textbook refers to . . .", "I think we veered off track . . ."

| Phatics, salutations | Communication that serves a purely social function: greetings, closures | "Hi all," "That's it for now," "We're having the most beautiful weather here" |

Source Adapted from Rourke et al., 1999

there are no serious personal challenges. Third, another very human way of establishing an interrelationship is through self-disclosure. Basically, the more we know about other members of the community, the more trustful and responsive we become.

Open Communication

Interpersonal communication has a direct effect on climate and open communication. Collaborative inquiry has as a foundation open communication that is reciprocal and respectful. Open communication requires a climate of trust and acceptance that allows questioning while protecting self-esteem and acceptance in the community. Open communication is built through a process of recognizing, complimenting, and responding to the questions and contributions of others, thereby encouraging reflective participation and interaction. Expressing agreement, as well as questioning the substance of messages, reveals engagement in the process of critical reflection and discourse. The inherently reflective and insightful communication in an e-learning community of inquiry is built upon open communication.

Cohesive Responses

Interpersonal and open communications contribute directly to the third category of social presence—group cohesion. Group cohesion is the dynamic state that social presence is attempting to achieve. It is cohesion that sustains the commitment and purpose of a community of inquiry, particularly in an e-learning group separated by time and space. More specifically, constructing meaning, confirming understanding, and completing collaborative activities can only be successfully achieved in a cohesive community. When students identify with the group and perceive themselves as part of a community of inquiry, the discourse, the sharing of meaning and the quality of learning outcomes will be optimized. Cohesive communication begins with activities such as addressing others by name. Group cohesion and association is taken to the next level by using inclusive pronouns such as "we" and "our."

Group cohesion creates an increased capacity to collaborate. The importance of group cohesion is supported by research (Baker, 2004; Conrad, 2005). It is recognized that group cohesion is predicated upon a delicate balance of personal and group identity. However, it is suggested that group identity be prioritized, recognizing that it serves to strengthen the community and interpersonal relationships take time to develop. Thus, social presence develops by attending to each of the categories concurrently but with the emphasis first on group identity (open communication and cohesion) while allowing the growth of personal affiliations.

PRACTICAL IMPLICATIONS

The fundamental question is: how does one establish social presence in an e-learning environment that will support a community of inquiry and concomitant, critically reflective discourse? The key to answering this question is recognizing that there may be an optimal level of social presence. Too little social presence may not sustain the community. On the other hand, too much social presence may inhibit disagreement and encourage surface comments and the distraction of social banter. After all, the primary goal is not social interaction and sustaining the group for personal reasons. The group sustained by social presence is a means to an end—the end being a quality learning experience for each and every student.

This issue of social presence supporting a larger purpose was brought to our attention by Liam Rourke, our research assistant, during research on this topic. Reflecting on the students, he stated:

> Despite theoretical rumors to the contrary, students do not complain that computer conferencing is asocial, terse, hostile, etc. On the contrary, if students complain, it is that the conference is too social, too polite, not critical or challenging, and thus not a productive learning experience.
>
> (Rourke, 2000, personal communication)

Therefore, from a social presence perspective, the greatest challenge in an e-learning context is to ensure a cognitively stimulating and productive learning environment. The criticism from students was that there was a "tone of decency" that translated into "warm feedback" and students not being challenged. A student summed up this "pathological politeness" phenomenon (a phrase coined by our colleague, Walter Archer) in the following manner:

> In the context of the [group], it was important to differentiate trust—a willingness to make oneself vulnerable to colleagues—from congeniality. The first is genuinely the basis for posing challenging questions; the latter can actually stand in the way of "straight talk."

This is a crucial distinction for the teacher when creating a community of inquiry and facilitating critical discourse. It is about gaining respect, not necessarily being liked.

More specifically, while these indicators have some empirical validity (Rourke, Anderson, Archer & Garrison, 1999), they are not all of equal importance in establishing social presence. For example, humor must be used carefully or it can isolate individuals. Due to the risk involved in using humor effectively in a lean, text-based medium, examples of humor are not commonly found in e-learning communities. Certainly, if it is to be used, it is perhaps best to wait until social presence is firmly established and the personalities of the individuals have been revealed sufficiently.

Another important factor in establishing social presence is the example set by the teacher. Modeling of appropriate messages and responses can be crucial in making students feel welcome and in giving them a sense of belonging. These messages and responses should set the tone and draw reluctant participants into the discussion. For this reason, the teacher or moderator must be particularly sensitive and responsive at the start of an e-learning experience. However, we must reiterate that the purpose of establishing a secure environment is to facilitate critical thinking and inquiry. Instructors should not emphasize personal identity at the expense of group identity and academic goals. Ice-breaking activities should not be focused only on introductions but designed around discussing course expectations and establishing group identity by asking students to collaboratively explore and negotiate requirements.

Finally, if possible, consideration needs to be given to an initial face-to-face or synchronous online meeting of the group. This can have an accelerating effect on establishing social presence and can shift the group dynamics much more rapidly toward intellectually productive activities. Learning activities that may be more effectively or efficiently conducted in a face-to-face setting could also be scheduled at this time. Such blended approaches have strong advantages that go beyond social presence. The downside is, of course, the loss of freedom with regard to independence of time. However, this may well be a worthwhile trade-off.

CONCLUSION

The previously described indicators can provide a pretty good sign of the level of social presence in a text-based e-learning community of inquiry. While strong social presence does provide the basis for respectful questioning and critique, it does not guarantee an optimally functioning community of inquiry. There must be an effective presence of the remaining elements of a community of inquiry—cognitive and teaching presence—to establish the optimal level of social presence for the specific educational context. It is the elements of cognitive and teaching presence that take a community beyond a largely social function to one of inquiry. To understand the transition of a group to the function of inquiry, we turn next to cognitive presence.

Chapter 5

Cognitive Presence

During the last decade the research focus on the Community of Inquiry theoretical framework has shifted from social presence to the challenge of engaging in an online inquiry process. Once we defined the cognitive presence construct (practical inquiry), the challenge was to understand how it functioned in an e-learning environment. From the inception of the cognitive presence concept, the question was whether higher-order thinking and discourse could be realized in an asynchronous text-based educational environment. More specifically, could cognitive presence be created in an online environment and could students successfully move through the phases of inquiry that defined cognitive presence? The goal in this chapter is to describe the cognitive presence model and provide an explanation of the nature and quality of practical inquiry conducted in an e-learning environment.

It is to the learning experience and the required cognitive presence that we focus our attention. We use the concept cognitive presence to describe the intellectual environment that supports sustained critical discourse and higher-order knowledge acquisition and application. More specifically, in the context of this discussion, cognitive presence means facilitating the analysis, construction, and confirmation of meaning and understanding within a community of learners through sustained discourse and reflection. In an e-learning context this includes being supported by primarily text-based communication.

CONCEPTUAL BACKGROUND

The theoretical context and framework for this discussion have been described previously in Chapters 2 and 3. The foundational framework is the CoI theoretical framework that is constituted by the three overlapping elements of social, teaching, and cognitive presence. In this section, we turn our attention to the genesis and manifestation of the cognitive presence concept.

CRITICAL THINKING

Cognitive presence is closely associated with the concept of critical thinking. The concept of critical thinking utilized here is derived from Dewey's (1933) reflective thinking model. For Dewey, reflective or critical thinking has practical value in that it deepens the meaning of our experiences and is, therefore, a core educational aim. The adjective "critical" is associated with "reasoning, evaluation and judgment, and these in turn have to do with the improvement of thinking" (Lipman, 2003, p. 3). Lipman also notes that critical thinking is sensitive to context in terms of exceptional circumstances and generalizability.

Critical thinking both authenticates existing knowledge and generates new knowledge which suggests an intimate connection with education. The other dimension that must be noted is the interplay between the private and public worlds. Lipman (2003) argues that the objective of the reflective paradigm is intellectual autonomy but, in reality, is "thoroughly social and communal" (p. 25). The importance of the concept of a community of inquiry in an educational context is supported by Lipman (2003) who states that "the reflective paradigm assumes education to be inquiry" (p. 19) and that the "only fully appropriate pedagogy [is] the community of inquiry approach" (p. 5). Inquiry is a self-correcting process where members of the community challenge beliefs and suggest alternative perspectives for exploration.

Critical or reflective thinking is integral to inquiry. However, what we mean by critical thinking is not self-evident. The reason, among others, for selecting Dewey's concept of reflective thinking is that it is comprehensive and coherent. Most forms of thinking (e.g., creative, critical, intuitive) can be interpreted within this framework (Garrison & Archer, 2000). Critical thinking is viewed here as an inclusive process of higher-order reflection and discourse. In an attempt to integrate various overlapping concepts associated with reflective and critical thinking, Garrison & Archer (2000) offer a generic model of critical thinking with its genesis in Dewey's phases of reflective thought that considers imagination, deliberation, and action (see Figure 5.1).

Perhaps the key element of this model is the overlay of the concept of the public and private worlds on the five phases. This is particularly relevant in an e-learning experience considering it is largely an asynchronous and text-based environment. In fact, a text-based environment has the potential to provide a remarkable balance between reflection and discourse. This is contrary to verbal discourse which is biased to a spontaneous and less reflective process. This recognition of two realities is an advantage in appreciating that while all phases have elements of reflection and discourse (unity principle), one phase may emphasize discourse over reflection and vice versa. Because reflection and discourse cannot be separated in practice, this distinction makes sense only in the abstract and is intended for purposes of analysis and understanding of inquiry and cognitive presence.

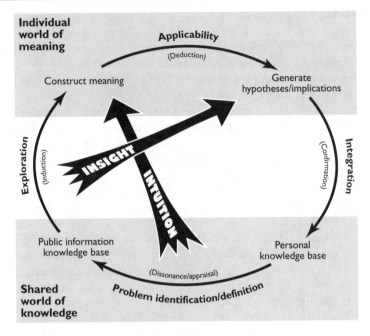

Figure 5.1 Critical Thinking and Intuition

The critical thinking model is useful in making sense of related concepts such as creative thinking, problem solving, intuition, and insight (Garrison & Archer, 2000). First, creative thinking is clearly a divergent process focused on the early stages of critical thinking. On the other hand, problem solving is mostly focused on convergent thinking that emphasizes the latter phase of the critical thinking process. That is, the goal is a solution to a specific problem. The differences between creative thinking and problem solving are a question of emphasis and purpose as both processes include elements of the other and are aspects of each of the critical thinking phases.

Secondly, concepts and processes related to intuition and insight cannot be ignored. These are important aspects of rational thought that can be explained and are not simply mystical processes to be rejected as unworthy of understanding. While there is an affective dimension to intuition and insight, they are important creative and subconscious inductive processes that are, according to Dewey, a "product of practical deliberation" (Garrison, J., 1997, p. 33). Intuition is not an "out of the blue" experience but is preceded by purpose and considerable reflective thinking. Moreover, like insight, it inevitably results from a deep and integrated understanding of a phenomenon. It is generally a vague, inexact awareness of the key to a problem that provides useful direction to explicate the solution clearly. This differs from insight in that insight is the classic "eureka" experience where clear solutions or coherent conceptualizations occur. While intuition arises more directly from experience, insight arises as a result of reflection (being immersed in a well-defined problem) and the generation of tentative conceptual representations (Garrison & Archer, 2000). Intuition and insight represent the union of perception and reason (Dewey, 1967) and are essential to coherent systematic thinking.

Educators seek to understand these cognitive processes in order to allow them to design more natural and less contrived educational experiences. That is, educational experiences that recognize how individuals reconstruct experience and construct meaning, thereby not simply condemning learners to assimilating inert knowledge. This is important in an e-learning context because of the cognitive freedom and control it affords the learner as well as recognizing the integration of the public (collaborative) and private (reflective) worlds. The collaborative yet reflective process of e-learning has great potential for facilitating critical thinking that is core to a worthwhile educational experience. The challenge is to use this to build the critical spirit along with discipline-specific, critical-thinking abilities developed through the process of constructing meaning and confirming understanding.

For purposes of simplicity, we define critical thinking in terms of practical inquiry (Garrison & Archer, 2000). Cognitive presence is seen to be defined and manifested through the Practical Inquiry (PI) model.

Practical Inquiry

Practical inquiry is grounded in experience (Dewey, 1933). The integration of the public and private worlds of the learner is a core concept in creating cognitive presence for educational purposes. The two-dimensional, PI model is presented in Figure 5.2. The continuum between *action–deliberation* is reflected in the vertical dimension of the model. This is consistent with the sociological (shared) and psychological (private) aspects of reflective thinking proposed by Dewey. As Dewey (1938) noted, "Any account of scientific method must be capable of offering a coherent doctrine of the nature of induction and deduction and of their relations to one another . . ." (p. 419). This dimension of practical inquiry is the rigorous process of integrating induction (arrival of generalizations) and deduction (employment of generalizations).

The transition between the concrete and abstract worlds is reflected in the *perception–conception* dimension of practical inquiry. This horizontal dimension reflects the point of fusion of the shared and private worlds. At one extreme is the divergent process of perception and analysis of facts or events. At the other extreme is the convergent process of insight and understanding associated with ideas and concepts. Therefore, the dimensions of the PI model reflect inductive/deductive and divergent/convergent processes of reflective or critical thinking core to the ideals of higher education.

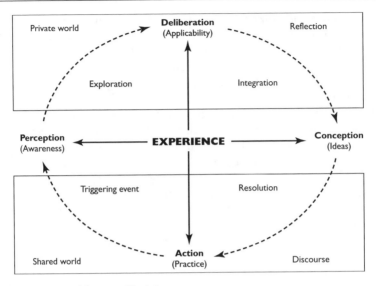

Figure 5.2 Practical Inquiry Model

Beyond the two basic dimensions of the model, practical inquiry includes four phases (trigger, exploration, integration, and resolution) that describe cognitive presence in an educational and e-learning context. To start, we must reiterate that these phases are not immutable. They are generalized guidelines that, in practice, may be "telescoped" or reversed as insight and understanding is either achieved or blocked. However, a metacognitive understanding of all phases can be of enormous value to both teacher and student in assessing the task at hand and progress achieved—not to mention metacognitive awareness and the ultimate goal of self-direction and learning to learn.

The first phase of practical inquiry is the initiation or triggering event. This needs to be a well-thought-out activity to ensure full engagement and buy-in from the students. It should also speak to a core organizing concept or issue of the knowledge domain being studied. Preferably, this would be a dilemma or problem that students could relate to from their experience or previous studies. While the responsibility of the teacher is to initiate this phase of task analysis, this can be structured in a more open manner by framing the issue and eliciting questions or problems that students see or have experienced. This has several positive outcomes in terms of involving students, assessing the state of knowledge, and generating unintended but constructive ideas.

The second phase of practical inquiry is exploration. This means first to understand the nature of the problem and then to search for relevant information and possible explanations. This may be done through group activities and brainstorming and/or through more private activities such as literature searches. Here students will experience iteration between the reflective and shared worlds as ideas are explored collaboratively and individuals try to make sense of what may seem to be complexity and confusion. This, however, is the essence of a true community of inquiry. The educational challenge is to monitor and regulate this phase of divergent thinking in such a way that it begins to be more focused in preparation for the next phase.

The third phase, integration, moves into a more focused and structured phase of constructing meaning. Decisions are made about integration of ideas and how order can be created parsimoniously. While this is a highly reflective phase, students are also intimately engaged in critical discourse that will shape understanding. It may be during this phase of the inquiry that the characteristics of e-learning come to the fore. The reflective and explicit nature of text-based communication may well facilitate deep and meaningful learning outcomes. For these very reasons, this is a particularly challenging phase for creating cognitive presence. In terms of assessing the depth or quality of learning outcomes, the teacher must probe for understanding and misconceptions as well as model the critical thinking process. The tendency is to become entrenched in the exploration phase and not move to more advanced phases of inquiry. Creating cognitive presence necessitates engaging students in all the phases of practical inquiry, including a metacognitive appreciation of the phases and challenges they are experiencing.

The fourth phase is the resolution of the dilemma or problem, whether that be reducing complexity by constructing a meaningful framework or discovering a contextually specific solution to a defined problem. This confirmation, or testing, phase may be accomplished by direct or vicarious action. Direct confirmation is more difficult and often impractical in an educational context. However, in an e-learning environment, with students operating out of work or family contexts, direct applications and testing may be more realistic. In any case, vicarious or mental modeling of solutions is a viable and worthwhile educational activity. In good educational environments, as in real life, resolution is seldom fully achieved. Inevitably, results of the resolution phase raise further questions and issues, triggering new cycles of inquiry and, thereby, encouraging continuous learning.

DEVELOPMENTS

Cognitive presence is at the core of a community of inquiry and also presents a serious challenge to support. The inherent reasons for this are the latent nature of learning as well as the asynchronous nature of the medium. However, a challenge that emerged early in this research was the apparent difficulty of moving discussion to the integration and resolution phases. In a previous review (Garrison & Arbaugh, 2007), arguments were presented that this was likely due to the fact that inquiry became more demanding as it moved to resolution; but, most importantly, this was explained as a function of teaching presence in terms of the design of the task (clear outcome expectation), the need to be more directive in providing crucial information, and moving the discussion forward in a timely manner. In this regard, although Rourke & Kanuka (2007) take a critical view of the advantages of online learning for critical discourse, they note in their study the importance of the teacher and the design in higher-order discourse and conclude that they observed "denser concentrations of postings in the higher phases of critical discourse models when students are presented with structured discussion activities with clearly defined roles for teachers and students" (p. 121).

This position has been supported in recent studies. In one large-scale study it was concluded that contrary to some previous research, "the vast majority of more than 5000 students in online and blended courses surveyed here reported that they achieved the highest levels of cognitive presence [practical inquiry] . . ." (Shea & Bidjerano, 2009b, p. 211). Other studies are more specific pointing to the design and nature of the task as the greatest factor in reaching resolution (Staley & Ice, 2009). Richardson & Ice (2010) found higher levels of practical inquiry "with 81% of students at the integration or resolution levels for the case-based strategy . . ." (p. 57). The conclusion is that tasks designed to achieve resolution will see greater activity at the integration and resolution phases (Stein, Wanstreet, Glazer, Engle, Harris, Johnston, Simons & Trinko, 2007). Finally, Bangert (2008) showed that teaching and social presence, in particular facilitation and direction, were associated with more messages at the highest levels (integration and resolution) of cognitive presence. Similarly, it was found that higher-order critical thinking (i.e., integration and solutions) could be produced in student discussions by specific instructional techniques (Pisutova-Gerber & Malovicova, 2009).

Insights associated with the phases of practical inquiry note that integration and resolution phases will naturally reflect fewer responses or contributions as participants are challenged and become more reflective when they converge on possible solutions (Akyol, Arbaugh, Cleveland-Innes, Garrison, Ice, Richardson & Swan, 2009). It should also be kept in mind that online discussions seldom provide sufficient time to reach resolution (Richardson & Ice, 2010). In this regard, one study increased activity at the integration and resolution phases by designating a specific and sufficient amount of time for discussion at each of the phases (de Leng, Dolmans, Jobsis, Muijtjens & van der Vleuten, 2009). Moreover, major projects generally reach resolution offline (Akyol & Garrison, 2008; Archer, 2010; Shea, Hayes, Vickers, Gozza-Cohen, Uzner, Mehta, Valchova & Rangan, 2010). With regard to major projects, Akyol & Garrison (in press a) noted that students believed they reached integration and resolution phases but "most of them thought that resolution is achieved individually through their final projects".

Cognitive presence has also been found to be associated with the nature of the course and the assignments. Perception of cognitive presence was significant for humanities and social sciences but not for professional courses requiring specific knowledge and skills (Garrison, Cleveland-Innes & Fung, 2010). A similar finding was reported by Arbaugh, Bangert & Cleveland-Innes (2010): these researchers "found significant disciplinary differences, particularly regarding cognitive presence, in soft, applied disciplines relative to other disciplines" (p. 37). More specifically, it was found that courses focusing on acquiring specific knowledge and skills, and the teacher informing the student, do not lend themselves to exploration and integration and, therefore, showed lower scores in cognitive presence (Arbaugh et al., 2010). Similarly, Gorsky, Caspi, Antonovsky, Blau & Mansur (2010) found that students in science courses with a large number of problem-solving assignments were more active, and levels of all presences were higher. From a teaching presence perspective, humanities' instructors posted three times more triggering messages while "science instructors posted four times as many messages associated with the category 'exploration'" (Gorsky et al., 2010, p. 64). Not only does this reflect possible differences in disciplines but also supports the importance of the nature of the task for cognitively engaging students.

Another area of cognitive presence research has focused on learning outcomes—both perceived and actual. Notwithstanding that cognitive presence is a process model, there has been some interest associated with its association to actual learning outcomes. This perspective has been a recent phenomenon but has created some misunderstanding (Akyol et al., 2009; Rourke & Kanuka, 2009). The question is whether the PI model can be used to measure learning outcomes. In this regard, it should be noted that the PI model has been compared to other models such as Bloom's taxonomy that measure learning outcomes with favorable results (Buraphadeja & Dawson, 2008; Cotton & Yorke, 2006; Meyer, 2004; Schrire, 2004, 2006). In fact, Schrire (2004) in comparing the PI model with Bloom's and the SOLO (structure of observed learning outcomes) taxonomies found the PI model "to be the most relevant to the analysis of the cognitive dimension and represents a clear picture of the knowledge-building processes occurring in online discussion" (p. 491). Buraphadeja & Dawson (2008) also note that the PI model has been widely cited as suitable for assessing critical thinking.

Perceived learning has been used as a proxy measure for learning outcomes due to the enormous challenge of validly measuring the quality of learning outcomes. While grades can be considered a measure of learning outcomes, too often they simply reflect a form of surface learning. That said, there is evidence that cognitive presence, as defined by the PI model, is associated with both perceived and actual learning outcomes (Akyol & Garrison, in press b; Benbunan-Fich & Arbaugh, 2006; Lim, Morris & Kupritz, 2007; Roblyer, Freeman, Donaldson & Maddox, 2007). The point is that perceived learning should not be discounted as a useful measure of learning, especially in the early stages of understanding the e-learning environment. To conclude this issue, while studying learning outcomes can provide important insights, outcomes need to be interpreted and inform the educational process. As Akyol et al. (2009) state: "The point is that understanding the educational transaction and processes of learning not only is the focus of the CoI framework but may well be of much greater value in understanding, shaping and improving the educational experience" (p. 9).

As was noted here and in Chapter 2, the CoI theoretical framework is a process model and each of the presences are dynamic and progressive. In particular, cognitive presence provides a model of how to approach learning in a constructivist manner. The explicit goal is to describe a process that is consistent with deep and meaningful approaches to learning. The primary focus is the process of constructing and confirming meaningful and worthwhile knowledge. While the process of practical inquiry is consistent with deep and meaningful learning outcomes, it remains focused on the expectation that the learning outcomes will be consistent with the goals of higher education.

A promising and worthwhile area of research that is just emerging in the context of e-learning is metacognition. Metacognition has been shown to be positively associated with academic achievement in face-to-face learning environments (Young & Fry, 2008), but little has been done in an asynchronous e-learning context. This area of study is of particular importance here as metacognition is core to successful inquiry. As Lipman (2003) notes, "All inquiry is self-critical practice . . ." (p. 83). Inquiry necessitates the knowledge and ability to monitor critically and regulate the learning process such that it is self-correcting. That is, to understand the inquiry process and what is required at each phase; then to exhibit the skills to ensure progression through the phases to resolution. This represents the iteration between monitoring and regulating the tasks and strategies in achieving intended learning outcomes.

Metacognition has been generally accepted as consisting of two components—awareness (knowledge) and implementation strategies (control). Awareness allows the learner to monitor the learning process and then to actively manage the inquiry process. In short, metacognition provides the knowledge and strategies to monitor and regulate effective inquiry. The challenge of studying metacognition in an e-learning context is that it requires a coherent theoretical framework. A study is currently ongoing using the CoI theoretical framework and the PI model to help understand the process of monitoring and regulating the inquiry process (Akyol & Garrison, unpublished).

Another line of research has shown that tagging discussion contributions encourages students to reflect on their thinking and "stimulates more in-depth and focused contributions (Schellens, Van Keer, De Wever & Valcke,

2009, p. 77). This technique can help to overcome the tendency of students to resist challenging arguments and being overly polite (Rourke & Kanuka, 2007). Similarly, labelling discussion contributions was also found to attain a higher level of cognitive processing which "mirrored a higher degree of metacognitive regulation in relation to planning, achieving clarity and monitoring" (Valcke, De Wever, Zhu & Deed, 2009, p. 165). This technique has value from both a research and practice perspective in understanding and promoting metacognition in an e-learning context.

Finally, an area of research associated with metacognition is that of motivation and expectations (Garrison & Archer, 2000). Motivation, as with metacognition, is manifested in terms of the convergence of each of the presences. For example, motivation is enhanced when social presence is addressed through trust, open communication and a sense of belonging (cohesion). It is also enhanced when teaching presence addresses expectations and provides guidance. Moreover, motivation is addressed as students' cognitive presence is enhanced through metacognitive awareness.

COGNITIVE PRESENCE DESCRIPTORS

Practical inquiry is the model within which we operationalize and assess cognitive presence. The goal is to provide a practical means to judge the nature and quality of critical reflection and discourse in a community of inquiry. The descriptors and indicators of cognitive presence generated in our research have considerable potential to assess the inquiry process. The goal is to use these indicators to assess critical thinking and discourse with regard to the developmental phases of practical inquiry. The goal of which is to facilitate discourse to achieve the greater purpose of achieving higher-order learning outcomes. In this regard, attention to process in terms of ensuring progression of reflection and discourse through to resolution is essential.

Table 5.1 provides the descriptors (adjectives characterizing process) and indicators (manifest examples) that correspond to each phase of the practical inquiry process. These were first based on the socio-cognitive processes that characterized each of the phases of practical inquiry. They were then enhanced and confirmed empirically (Garrison, Anderson & Archer, 2001).

The first phase, the triggering event, is associated with conceptualizing a problem or issue. For this reason we consider this evocative and inductive by nature. The educational processes would include presenting information that generates curiosity and questions. It should also further discussion in a way that builds into subsequent phases of inquiry. An example might be a statement and question such as: "It has been argued that the only way to deliver effective e-learning is through a Community of Inquiry model or approach. Why do you think that is?"

Table 5.1 Practical Inquiry Descriptors and Indicators

Phase	Descriptor	Indicator
Triggering event	Evocative (inductive)	Recognize problem Puzzlement
Exploration	Inquisitive (divergent)	Divergence Information exchange Suggestions Brainstorming Intuitive leaps
Integration	Tentative (convergent)	Convergence Synthesis Solutions
Resolution	Committed (deductive)	Apply Test Defend

The second phase, exploration, is a search for relevant information and ideas. For this reason, this is an inquisitive and divergent process. The educational process would include: brainstorming ideas; offering supportive or contradictory ideas and concepts; soliciting narratives of relevant perspectives or experiences; and eliciting comments or responses as to the value of the information or ideas. Following the previous theme, a typical statement corresponding to the exploration phase might be: "One reason I think learning communities are seldom used is that it is too complicated to get co-operation. Another may be the mindset of those in charge to change practices."

The third phase, integration, is the process of constructing a meaningful solution or explanation. Therefore, this is considered to be a tentative connection of ideas capable of meeting defined criteria, providing meaning, and offering potential solutions. The educational transaction would include: integrating information; offering messages of agreement; building on other ideas; providing a rationale or justification; and explicitly offering a solution. An example would be: "We also had trouble getting co-operation. Often the use of new tools requires new organizational structures. We addressed these issues when we implemented a systems approach, and I think that's why we were successful."

The fourth phase, resolution, critically assesses the viability of the proposed solution through direct or vicarious application. Resolution requires a commitment to test the solution deductively, perhaps through vicarious implementation or thought experiment. This would require a rigorous analysis of the hypothetical test, which could take the form of a presentation and defense with other participants critiquing the suggested application. On the other hand, the test could take the form of a direct application or action research project—either an individual or group project. An example of an exchange consistent with this phase of practical inquiry might be: "A good test would be to ensure that participants understand the expectations, and that collaboration is properly rewarded. Once implemented, this could be assessed by considering project grades as well as the impressions of the participants."

As revealed in recent research, the challenge for educators is to move the discussion and individual cognitive development through each of the phases of practical inquiry. That is, to build the discussion from problem recognition (triggering event) through to exploration, integration, and resolution. The tendency is to do the first two phases very well, the third phase less well, and the last phase hardly at all. As discussed previously, this is very likely due to the nature of the task and lack of a teaching presence moving the discussion forward. There must be an appreciation and commitment to the value of thinking progressively through a problem and dilemma such that some worthwhile and long-term benefit ensues. This, of course, is the essential purpose of an educational experience.

What is most required to create cognitive presence and higher-order learning outcomes consistent with intended goals and expectations of the educational experience is a moderator who can assess qualitatively the nature of the discourse and then proactively shape it following the critical thinking cycle. Considering the somewhat ethereal nature of e-learning, it is important that participants be encouraged to relate the ideas and concepts to societal contexts. This will focus the discourse on integration and resolution. Moreover, the likelihood of this progressive development of the cognitive process happening is greatly enhanced with a metacognitive understanding of critical thinking and practical inquiry (i.e., cognitive presence). It may also be extremely helpful to creating cognitive presence for all the participants to also have a metacognitive appreciation of what they are doing and why.

CONCLUSION

Cognitive presence operationalized through the Practical Inquiry model provides insight into the cognitive aspects of an e-learning experience and a means to assess the qualitative nature of that discourse. In turn, assessing the nature of the discourse can provide insights into the nature of the teaching and learning transaction and what interventions may be appropriate. While much work remains to refine this tool empirically, the PI model with its indicators is a good heuristic method of guiding and assessing the nature and quality of cognitive presence. A quantitative method of assessing cognitive presence based on this model can be found in the CoI survey (see Appendix).

Chapter 6

Teaching Presence

Because of expanded educational opportunities and choices, teaching in an e-learning context is an onerous responsibility. The e-learning environment extends interaction and this has a liberating but transformational effect on approaches to teaching. To be constrained by the restricted frame of traditional classroom presentational approaches is to ignore the capabilities and potential of e-learning. Implicit in this recognition is the need to rethink the purpose, approach, and nature of the educational transaction. Despite the challenges associated with designing and delivering a meaningful and worthwhile learning experience, it is clear that the technologies associated with e-learning provide enormous opportunities and choice for connection and reflection that cannot be ignored.

With the expanded capabilities and choices that e-learning presents, there has been a shift toward a collaborative inquiry-based approach associated with critical thinking and discourse. This is a learning-centerd approach rather than a learner-centered approach. From a formal learning or educational perspective this distinction is more than a subtlety or nuance. Education is a unified process where teachers and students have important, complementary responsibilities. The focus is on learning, but not just whatever the learner capriciously decides. An educational experience is intended to focus on learning outcomes that have societal value as well as the ability for the individual to continue learning. A learner-centered approach risks marginalizing the teacher and the value of creating an educational community of inquiry. In an educational experience, both the learner and teacher are part of the larger process of learning. Teaching presence is charged with shaping the appropriate transactional balance and, along with the learners, managing and monitoring the achievement of worthwhile learning outcomes in a timely manner.

In most cases, simply reassigning responsibility and control to the learner violates the intent and integrity of the educational experience to facilitate a critical and constructive learning process. Teaching presence performs an essential service in identifying relevant societal knowledge, designing experiences that will facilitate reflection and discourse, and diagnosing and assessing learning outcomes. With e-learning, this is both easier and more difficult. It is easier in the sense that the e-learning medium supports sustained and reflective dialogue. It is more difficult, however, in that this medium is inherently different and requires new approaches.

To establish appropriate teaching presence, it is necessary to go beyond fragmented suggestions or techniques of e-learning. More effort and creativity must go into understanding and appreciating the integrating element of teaching presence to facilitate critical thinking and higher-order learning outcomes within an e-learning context.

ROLES AND FUNCTIONS

The role of the teacher in an e-learning community of inquiry must change—but for the better. In its best sense, the core principles and responsibilities of a traditional educational transaction are translatable to an e-learning context. While effective teaching can take different forms, principles such as clear expectations, critical discourse, and diagnosis of misconceptions are common to both face-to-face and e-learning environments. The responsibilities of teaching in any context are complex and multi-faceted. They include being a subject matter expert, an educational designer, a facilitator, and a teacher. However, as has been noted, the liberating frame of e-learning significantly alters how these responsibilities are fulfilled.

There is remarkable consistency across the literature as to the categories of teaching presence associated with an e-learning context. Although there is some shifting of roles across the categories, there is a close mapping of the classification schemes associated with e-learning and the three categories of teaching presence adopted here. Table 6.1 demonstrates the consistency of the various teaching roles across each of the references. These are reasonably intuitive but also have some empirical support (Anderson, Rourke, Garrison & Archer, 2001; Rossman, 1999). The intuitiveness and consistency of these elements provide confidence and understanding upon which to explore further and explicate teaching presence in an e-learning context.

As noted in Table 6.1, the educator's roles fall into three primary categories: design and organization; facilitation; and direct instruction. Consistent with this, we define teaching presence as "the design, facilitation, and direction of cognitive and social processes for the purpose of realizing personally meaningful and educationally worthwhile learning outcomes" (Anderson et al., 2001, p. 5). From this description, there should be no doubt as to the essential role teaching presence plays in integrating the various elements of an educational experience made ever more challenging in an e-learning context.

Before describing each of the elements of teaching presence, it should be emphasized that teaching presence is what participants (usually the

Table 6.1 Teaching Roles in E-Learning

Anderson et al.	Berge	Paulsen	Mason
Instructional design and organization	Managerial	Organizational	Organizational
Facilitation	Social	Social	Social
Direct instruction	Pedagogical Technical	Intellectual	Intellectual

instructor) do to create a community of inquiry that includes both cognitive and social presence. Therefore, we do not focus specifically on the social and cognitive elements themselves but on the roles of a teacher or the actual functions that a teacher must perform to create and maintain a dynamic learning environment. These functions are integrative in the sense that teaching presence must bring together the cognitive and social in purposeful and synergistic ways. It will be noted that there is properly a cognitive bias in terms of educational purpose and that social presence is an important but mediating element.

Identifying more precisely indicators and corresponding examples for each of the teaching presence categories can provide useful guidelines, especially for those less familiar with e-learning methods. Detailed descriptions of each of the three elements of teaching presence follow.

DESIGN AND ORGANIZATION

Design and organization has to do with macro-level structure and process. Perhaps not surprisingly, the design and organization of an e-learning course of studies is, at least initially, more demanding than the design and organization of a similar course of studies in a face-to-face only classroom environment. This is due, first, to the technology and the need for teachers to redesign approaches to teaching and learning to maximize the capabilities of the e-learning medium. Secondly, this redesign may be a considerable undertaking for those who have, in the past, relied exclusively on lecturing. For these individuals there will be a greater need to focus on the design and organizational element of teaching in adjusting to an e-learning community of inquiry context. This new approach will likely be further compounded by the fact that some students will not have experienced an e-learning course, and new expectations and behaviors will require understanding and patience.

Building the curriculum is made more complex by having to deal with the apparent contradiction of having both to increase and decrease content. That is, content is increased in the sense of providing links to other sites that may include important learning objects or supplementary material; and decreased

Table 6.2 Instructional Design and Organization Indicators

Indicators	Examples
Setting curriculum	"This week we will be discussing . . ."
Designing methods	"I am going to divide you into groups, and you will debate . . ."
Establishing time parameters	"Please post a message by Friday . . ."
Utilizing medium effectively	"Try to address issues that others have raised when you post"
Establishing netiquette	"Keep your messages short"
Making macro-level comments about course content	"This discussion is intended to give you a broad set of tools/skills which you will be able to use in deciding when and how to use different research techniques"

in the sense that, if there is to be considerable interactivity, reducing the quantity of material presented cannot be ignored. In conjunction with this broadening and channeling of course materials is the crucial task of selecting collaborative activities and assignments. It is here that an understanding of the medium of e-learning intersects with the actual teaching and learning transaction. The design work at the front end of a course of studies will pay considerable dividends during the course of study. It will not, however, preclude organizational decisions throughout the inquiry process. Table 6.2 provides the design indicators along with exemplars.

Design and organizational responsibilities provide the structure for any learning experience and have similar responsibilities and functions. The semantic difference is that design refers to structural decisions made before the process begins, while organization refers to similar decisions that are made to adjust to changes during the educational transaction (i.e., *in situ* design). Organizational comments reflect the flexible and non-prescriptive nature of any educational experience. Design is but a flexible template, created with the expectation that specific issues and needs will inevitably arise that will necessitate organizational changes in the course of action.

The collaborative nature of a community of inquiry places an increased importance on organizational issues. The indeterminate nature of the entry and development of knowledge in students will inevitably introduce some uncertainty into the design process. If e-learning is to be a collaborative constructivist process, then students must have some influence in what is studied and how it is approached. Therefore, design should not be separated from delivery. It continues in the guise of organizational responsibilities and, as such, there are considerable advantages to ensuring continuity from the design to the organization phase. This is best accomplished when both design and organization allow for effective responsiveness to developing needs and events.

FACILITATING DISCOURSE

The second element of teaching presence, facilitating reflection and discourse for the purpose of building understanding, goes to the heart of the e-learning experience. Facilitating discourse recognizes the role of the community of inquiry as enabling and encouraging the construction of personal meaning as well as shaping and confirming mutual understanding. This element represents the fusion of purpose, process, and outcome. It is where interest, engagement, and learning converge.

Teaching presence plays an essential role in facilitating discourse in an e-learning experience. Managing and monitoring discourse in an e-learning context is no less important than in face-to-face discussions. The reflective and rigorous nature of text-based communication demands serious commitment but presents opportunities for deep and meaningful learning. To sustain this commitment and encourage quality contributions requires that the discourse be focused and productive.

Teaching presence responsibilities require sustained attention to a broad range of issues. The overriding concern is to establish and sustain the learning community to ensure progression toward intended educational goals. This demands attention to both cognitive and social presence concerns. Postings must be closely monitored and the nature and timing of responses must be carefully considered. In addition, the community must be somewhat self-sustaining and self-correcting; therefore, too little or too much teaching presence may adversely affect the discourse and the process of building understanding. While maintaining this balance, teacher postings must model critical discourse while shaping the discussion to achieve purposeful goals. Guidance is also required to engage less responsive students as well as curtail the exuberance of those who will inevitably tend to dominate the discussion. These skills are not so different from facilitating a face-to-face discussion.

At the same time, the challenge is not simply to encourage or reward prolific responses. Teaching presence must encourage appropriate and relevant responses by bring attention to well-reasoned responses and making linkages to other messages. Participants must feel the discussion is moving in a purposeful direction and in a timely manner. The threads of the discussion need to be brought together and shared understanding explicitly stated. All of this requires more than a "guide on the side" but less than a "sage on the stage." That is, the teacher must negotiate something more substantial than a rambling conversation yet not just a prescriptive dissemination of information. When students begin to take responsibility to construct collaboratively and confirm understanding, teaching presence has found the

Table 6.3 Facilitating Discourse Indicators

Indicators	Examples
Identifying areas of agreement/disagreement	"Joe, Mary has provided a compelling counter-example to your hypothesis. Would you care to respond?"
Seeking to reach consensus/understanding	"I think Joe and Mary are saying essentially the same thing"
Encouraging, acknowledging, or reinforcing student contributions	"Thank you for your insightful comments"
Setting climate for learning	"Don't feel self-conscious about 'thinking out loud' on the forum. This is a place to try out ideas after all"
Drawing in participants, prompting discussion	"Any thoughts on this issue?" "Anyone care to comment?"
Assess the efficacy of the process	"I think we're getting a little off track here"

appropriate balance of control. Indicators and examples of facilitating discourse are shown in Table 6.3.

Facilitating discourse for purposes of building understanding involves pedagogical, interpersonal, and organizational issues. Teaching presence must be as concerned with cognitive development as with a positive learning environment, and it must see content, cognition, and context as integral parts of the whole. However, some messages are primarily social, occur in chat rooms, and are generally off-limits to the teacher. Other contributions are more complex and embed various cognitive and social elements. This is where the full responsibility of facilitation comes to bear.

DIRECT INSTRUCTION

Direct instruction goes beyond that of a facilitation role and is most often associated with specific content issues, such as diagnosing misconceptions. Scholarly leadership manifests itself in this situation and is often quite specific in nature. Although this is a legitimate and important authoritative influence, this essential teaching responsibility has often been either ignored or downgraded in an e-learning context. Disciplinary expertise and efficient shaping of the learning experience are essential aspects of any educational process. The risk in e-learning is that the proper educational and intellectual climate and direction may be lost.

The need for direct instruction challenges the "guide on the side" concept. While the concept of a guide or facilitator is integral to teaching presence, in and of itself it is limited as an educational approach to e-learning. It suggests

Table 6.4 Direct Instruction Indicators

Indicators	Examples
Present content/questions	"Bates says . . . what do you think"
Focus the discussion on specific issues	"I think that's a dead end. I would ask you to consider . . ."
Summarize the discussion	"The original question was . . . Joe said . . . Mary said . . . we concluded that . . . We still haven't addressed . . ."
Confirm understanding through assessment and explanatory feedback	"You're close, but you didn't account for . . . this is important because . . ."
Diagnose misconceptions	"Remember, Bates is speaking from an administrative perspective, so be careful when you say . . ."
Inject knowledge from diverse sources, e.g., textbook, articles, Internet, personal experiences (includes pointers to resources)	"I was at a conference with Bates once, and he said . . . You can find the proceedings from the conference at http://www . . ."
Responding to technical concerns	"If you want to include a hyperlink in your message, you have to . . ."

an artificial separation of facilitator and content expert, and speaks to the potential distortion of an educational experience that has become pathologically focused on student-centeredness to the exclusion of the influence of a pedagogical and content expert. Such a laissez-faire approach misinterprets the collaborative constructivist approach to learning and the importance of systematically building learning experiences (i.e., scaffolding) to achieve intended, higher-order learning experiences.

Teaching presence is not possible without the expertise of an experienced and responsible teacher who can identify the ideas and concepts worthy of study, provide the conceptual order, organize learning activities, guide the discourse, offer additional sources of information, diagnose misconceptions, and interject when required. These are direct and proactive interventions that support an effective and efficient learning experience. Indicators and examples of direct instruction are shown in Table 6.4.

DEVELOPMENTS

The evidence attesting to the importance of teaching presence has grown considerably since the first edition of this book (Garrison & Arbaugh, 2007; Garrison, Cleveland-Innes & Fung, 2010; Shea & Bidjerano, 2009a). This research has consistently reported the importance of teaching presence for perceived learning and satisfaction (Akyol & Garrison, in press b). The importance of an instructor's support and expertise was shown to be very important for the acquisition of knowledge (Paechter, Maier & Macher, 2010). Interaction and discourse play an essential role in a community of inquiry and it has been shown that teaching presence is crucial to ensure participation and quality of responses (An, Shin & Lim, 2009; Bliss & Lawrence, 2009; Gorsky, Caspi, Antonovsky, Blau & Mansur, 2010). Instructors who support and moderate communication were also found to support community development (Brook & Oliver, 2007). Similarly, Shea, Li & Pickett (2006) concluded that strong teaching presence "is related both to students' sense of connectedness and learning" (p. 85). Teaching presence is also associated with a sense of community (Ice, Curtis, Phillips & Wells, 2007; Perry & Edwards, 2005; Shea et al., 2006). Finally, an interesting finding that should be studied further is that students turn to instructors for help in difficult distance education courses but not in moderately difficult or easy courses (Gorsky, Caspi & Smidt, 2007).

An aspect that has only recently been addressed is in understanding the changes in emphasis of the categories of teaching presence over the duration of a course of studies. Insight into this phenomenon was initially reported by Vaughan & Garrison (2006) when they found that design and facilitation comments decreased over time while direct instruction comments increased considerably. This pattern was confirmed when it was found that direct instruction increased significantly over time (Akyol & Garrison, 2008). As with social and cognitive presence, more research is required into the dynamics of the presences as a course develops over time.

The teaching presence construct has been confirmed by a number of studies (Garrison & Arbaugh, 2007; Ke, 2010). However, a question has been raised about the stability of its dimensions. In particular, Shea et al. (2006) conducted a factor analysis of over 2,000 college students and concluded that a two-factor solution was most interpretable. The results did not appear to distinguish between facilitation and direct instruction. On the other hand, another study suggested that students may view design and direct instruction similarly (Arbaugh, Cleveland-Innes, Diaz, Garrison, Ice, Richardson, Shea & Swan, 2008). To be clear, these studies can be explained from two perspectives. Teaching presence categories are interdependent variables and the particular sample of students may not fully appreciate the distinction among the responsibilities associated with teaching presence. Considering these two factors together it may not be surprising that there may be difficulties in distinguishing these dimensions.

Considering the importance of teaching presence it is a bit surprising that this is perhaps the least studied presence. There is still much to understand from both a theoretical and practical perspective regarding teaching presence and its interaction with the social and cognitive presences in a dynamic community of inquiry.

CONCLUSION

The categories of teaching presence provide a template that can be of considerable value to designing, facilitating, and directing an e-learning experience. Notwithstanding the essential role of a teacher, it needs to be emphasized that in the CoI framework, all participants have the opportunity to contribute to teaching presence. In fact, if the ultimate goal is to learn to learn, students must be encouraged to become critical thinkers and be self-directed in monitoring and regulating their learning appropriate to the task and their ability. This becomes even more obvious when we suggest designating student moderators. For these reasons, we have not referred to this concept as *teacher* presence but rather as *teaching* presence. As participants develop cognitively and socially, the more distributed teaching presence will become. At the same time, who assumes the role does not diminish the importance of teaching presence in creating and sustaining a community of inquiry.

To this point we have provided the framework and elements of an e-learning experience. We have not attempted to identify principles or suggest specific guidelines with regard to the practice of e-learning. This means thinking differently about what an e-learning experience can be. It means recognizing the possibility of creating a community of inquiry that challenges and builds upon others' ideas. A community of inquiry necessitates that we conceive of the role of the teacher not in a diminished but in a different presence.

Part II

Applying the CoI
Theoretical Framework

Chapter 7

Instructional Technologies

Instructional technologies are playing a crucial enabling role in the transformation of teaching and learning in higher education. These technologies have become the catalyst to rethinking the teaching and learning transaction. Educators are realizing that new and emerging communications technologies are radically changing the educational landscape in terms of flexibility and connectivity. They are providing the means to create fully engaged communities of learners independent of time and space. These technological innovations are not exotic or expensive; they are technologies that have permeated most aspects of life in our increasingly connected society. The ability to connect instructors and students in a sustained manner has changed the expectations and approaches to teaching and learning in higher education.

It is important to appreciate that instructional technologies make possible the transformation of the educational experience. Instructional technology directly influences the display, the interaction, the cost, and the design of educational outcomes. However, technological innovation should be first and foremost about improving the effectiveness of the educational transaction. It is to this purpose that technological innovation represents the core of the theory and practice of e-learning. The influence of e-learning in higher education has and will continue to be driven by a focus on enhancing the teaching and learning transaction. That is, the ability to create and sustain discourse and precipitate reflection in a community of learners.

HISTORICAL PERSPECTIVE

Historically, the word technology referred to the systematic approach to a craft. This original emphasis on systematic treatment and an implied adherence to tenants of science has inspired the field of instructional technology to embrace a scientific view of its activities. The more common understanding of technology, however, is that it is a tool as opposed to a systematic process or technique. It can be confusing when we label all systematic designs, thoughts, expressions, and plans as technologies. Therefore, for our purposes here we will distinguish the technology as a tool from the academic process.

Notwithstanding this distinction, it is limiting to analyze a technological tool outside of the ways in which that tool is applied. In an educational context, instructional technology implies a discussion of the way in which a tool is used as well as the characteristics, limitations, and applications of that tool. That is, instructional technology must be seen as a means to access information and support communication within a community of learners. This focus on the technological tools, therefore, should not be separated from the mindful application of these tools in a purposeful educational context.

Instructional technology as a field of study came into its own in the 1960s. With this came many technological innovations that had little influence on instructional practices, at least not until the Internet and the World Wide Web emerged in the 1990s. Looking back, the Internet represented a sea change in the widespread adoption of communications technology and how we view technology generally. Educators have begun to understand that technology is not just a neutral delivery vehicle. New technologies possess characteristics that are changing the educational paradigm and influencing the quality of the learning experience. The unanticipated impact of the Internet has set the stage for the rapid development of e-learning.

Perhaps the first significant disruption caused by e-learning capabilities and approaches is in the field of distance education. Traditionally, the practice of distance education lay in coping with the challenge of access through independent study. This reality was solidified through Peters' (2007) industrial model of distance education characterized by division of labor, mass production, and economies of scale. The great success of this approach was the access and efficiencies gained through adopting industrialized economies of scale. The downside was the depersonalization of the educational process that required students "to become autonomous and self-regulated with regard to goals, methods, and media . . ." (Peters, 2007, p. 61).

The principles and practices of distance education as a self-paced and independent form of learning have been seriously questioned as a result of developments in e-learning. The flexible and collaborative potential of e-learning is in stark contrast to the traditional practices of distance education. There are questions as to whether distance education can or will be reformed in light of the growth of research and practice associated with e-learning (Cleveland-Innes & Garrison, 2010; Garrison, 2009a). Moreover, with the convergence of face-to-face and online learning (blended learning), will this further marginalize traditional distance education with its preoccupation with access and its commitment to independent study? It is not clear whether traditional distance education and its industrial paradigm will be relegated to the scrap yard and its useful parts recycled (Evans & Pauling, 2010).

Miller (2010) argues that distance education is being redefined by e-learning. He states that "Online learning is both a symptom of the changes in the broader society and a tool of transformation" (12th paragraph). He goes on to say that online learning is a tool of transformation and as higher education responds a new pedagogy is emerging—a pedagogy that is based on a changing sense of community and is inquiry based. This pedagogy that Miller refers to is the Community of Inquiry theoretical framework. As a result, online learning is blurring the distinctions between online and campus-based learning, and distance education in the form of online communities of inquiry is moving into the mainstream of higher education.

E-LEARNING TECHNOLOGIES

The task of scholars is to create conceptual models that allow us to better understand the world we inhabit and create. A core concept in the quest for educational models is the realization that the essence of education is communication. It is the way technology is used to support academic communication that best describes educational practice. This perspective will help us to place in context the technology of e-learning.

Historically, the focus of distance education on access and economies of scale shifted attention away from two-way communication and interaction. On the other hand, e-learning has had just the opposite effect. This is understandable as we appreciate that the antecedents of e-learning are associated with computer conferencing and, before that, it had its roots in computer-assisted learning, educational psychology, and instructional technologies. In addition, from a learning perspective, e-learning has as its theoretical foundation collaborative constructivist approaches to learning. E-learning has carried forward this commitment to engage students collaboratively in sustainable communities of inquiry.

E-learning is less about issues of access and bridging distances than it is about creating communities of learners independent of time and space (Garrison, 2009a). This represents a radical shift in core assumptions, goals, and practices. The great advance of e-learning was to clearly demonstrate that with new communications technologies, interaction and independence were not mutually exclusive. It was no longer a zero-sum game in that educators could design collaborative learning experiences while maintaining flexibility and independence. This was made possible with the advent of the Internet and a wide range of communications technologies. Despite the great fanfare and enthusiasm for various technological innovations over the years, instructional technologies have not had a significant impact on mainstream higher education. That is, not until the emergence of e-learning.

To reiterate, e-learning is more than just a form of distance education. The acceptance of e-learning has been associated with its ability to create communities of inquiry either at a distance or blended with campus-based instruction. In this way e-learning has transcended the notion that it was just an efficient means to deliver course materials or a lecture. E-learning has shifted the thinking of distance and campus-based educators in significant ways. Some of the new technologies that have been the catalyst for this rethinking are described next.

WEB 2.0

The first decade of this century saw the emergence of what has been termed Web 2.0 technologies that give greater flexibility to the user to communicate and control information. From an educational perspective, the key to the adoption of instructional technologies for e-learning is to recognize their potential to support collaborative constructivist approaches to teaching and learning. Notwithstanding the enormous potential of Web 2.0 technologies for collaboration, we need to take a close look at these tools as they apply to specific tasks. To assess these technologies for educational purposes, it is extremely helpful to have a coherent framework to help make sense of their impact socially, cognitively, and pedagogically.

The administrative backbone of e-learning has been the course management system (CMS). This software provides a wide range of tools to support e-learning. More specifically, the CMS provides a means to organize and deliver content as well as support assignments, discussion boards, and assessment. Course management systems are also capable of providing the platform for any number of other Web 2.0 tools. Two of the more popular tools used in e-learning contexts are blogs and wikis. A blog is a website for the purposes of discussion and sharing relevant content. In an educational context a blog can be a site maintained by a student that invites comments from peers that, in turn, encourages personal reflection. A wiki is similar to a blog except that it provides for the collaborative creation of documents and editing of content. An educational application would be team projects, and to summarize online discussions collaboratively.

Notwithstanding the educational benefits of tools like blogs and wikis, the reality is that students are skeptical about the use of blogs, wikis, and social networks (Hartshorne & Ajjan, 2009) should create pause for thought for educators. It is highly unlikely that faculty will be any more open to the use of these tools unless the educational value is clearly understood. For these reasons, there is much work to be done on how to use these tools effectively in an integrated educational experience.

Social Media

We use the term social media to apply to specific applications that support social networking and build relationships (e.g., Facebook) through the creation of personal profiles and the ability to add and interact with friends.

It is a means to share recent activities, photos, and thoughts with selected friends. Another application is a form of blogging that allows subscribers to send short messages on a particular topic (e.g., Twitter). The focus here is more on sharing information and opinion than on social networking. The risk is superficial and less sustained thinking. Regardless, both these applications have gained worldwide popularity. The challenge for educators is to understand what is meant by social networking and the value it might add to an educational experience.

Based on the widespread popularity of social media, social networking such as Twitter has entered the mythical phase. This is the phase where the power and impact of the technology is hyped to a point that there will be inevitable disenchantment. With regard to social media, however, this necessitates a critical view to understand what place they might have in the world of higher education. At this time, however, we need to take a serious look at social media and understand how these applications can benefit higher education. On the surface, examples of social networking such as Twitter with its requirement for extremely short messages certainly suggest a high degree of spontaneity and superficiality. On the other hand, education is the antithesis of superficiality and it begs the question whether higher education risks superficiality with the uncritical adoption of social software and networking such as Twitter and Facebook?

Social media and networking do not translate in a one-to-one manner to effective collaborative learning experiences. While social learning is part of a community of inquiry, it is not synonymous with collaborative constructivist approaches to deep and meaningful learning processes and outcomes. While students may be open to the use of social media in the classroom, there is a "significant difference between the perceived role of this tool [Facebook] as social, rather than educational" (Roblyer, McDaniel, Webb, Herman & Witty, 2010, p. 138). As such, it is unclear at this point whether social media have a significant role to play in mainstream higher education. Higher education is about the context and process of worthwhile learning. The reality is that there is little evidence as to the benefit and learning effectiveness of social networking. As Sanger (2010, p. 18) states:

> There is no reason to think that repurposing social media for education will magically make students more inspired and engaged.

Sanger goes on to say that what engages people about social media is the passion for their personal interests and to stay in touch with friends. And to the heart of the matter, Sanger (2010) asks, "is fostering a deeply networked online social life among the proper tasks of education . . .?" (p. 22) This should cause serious educators and researchers to pause to think about the role of social media in higher education. At what point does condensing a message result in dumbing down discourse? When is context and meaning lost? While the role of social media in higher education must be approached with caution, it is suggested that the CoI theoretical framework can provide the conceptual order to sort through the issues of social networking and proper social presence that is an important mediating variable between teaching and cognitive presence and its contribution to student satisfaction (Garrison, Cleveland-Innes & Fung, 2010).

Certainly it is too early to tell how the ubiquity and current popularity of social media will impact educational environments. However, at a purely social level, there may well be added value of social media in creating and sustaining learning communities. For example, there is evidence that students who are satisfied with the campus climate also persist (Schreiner, 2009). The argument is that if students feel connected and part of the larger community, they will be happier and persist. Not only might social networking contribute to social presence in the classroom, but it could become an important ingredient in campus life for those commuter institutions where students spend so little time on campus. If social media help students persist and be successful, then this technology will find a place in higher education. At the same time, assessing the educational value and specific applications of these emerging technologies needs considerable study.

Mobile Learning

Very much related to social media are mobile technologies. These include a wide range of devices from laptops to cell phones. They go hand in hand with social networking and the ability to send email, access the web, and record audio and video from any location. However, the application of mobile technologies in higher education is only just being considered. There are issues with the technology in terms of the type of device (cell, pads, laptop), standard file formats, reliability, and cost of service (ownership). For example, it may be technically difficult or costly sending and receiving large amounts of data. This is where educational and student needs must take precedent.

Mobile devices can be used for a range of educational purposes such as podcasts or taking a quiz. However, the question is whether these are best used for more complex tasks that require concentrated reflection. As with social networking, the question is the educational value-add of communication on the go. While there may be educational value in connecting individuals socially, the question is whether mobile communication technology is a good application for academic communication and discourse?

A recent study has provided an important perspective on the use of mobile devices compared to accessing course materials and activities online using desktop computers and a learning management system (LMS) (Koole, McQuilkin & Ally, 2010). The researchers asked what is the reality of mobile learning? Notwithstanding the arguments for more freedom and increased connectedness, the study concluded that "respondents may not consider mobile access as important as basic desktop computer access to their LMS" (Koole et al., 2010, p. 73). More telling, students felt that mobile access did not increase their sense of connectedness and rated studying through a mobile system extremely low. In assessing the reality of mobile devices the question is what value does it add to current desktop LMS access? Speculation here is that mobile devices may have real value in specific contexts, such as the health profession, where immediate access to information and guidance would be a great asset.

The need for a cautious approach to technologies such as mobile devices is expressed well in an ELI (2010) resource. It is stated that "applications used in mobile learning generally focus on brief interactions . . . [and] enable the quick review of information rather than prolonged deep learning . . ." (2nd paragraph). While there are legitimate uses of mobile devices, the reality is that most of these situations do not lend themselves to the type of sustained educational discourse and reflection described here in an educational community of inquiry. Participating in a reflective discussion using a cell phone in a public setting may not be a strong argument for mobile learning. In this regard, Brown & Diaz (2010) make the point that smart phone use by undergraduates is for short-term applications, as it is hard to imagine typing a lengthy message or document using the keyboard of a highly mobile device such as a smart phone. At this point, the best argument for mobile devices would appear to be rapid access to, or recording of, information in a field situation.

Some argue that portable communication devices could provide an opportunity for communication within the classroom. Here mobile devices can be used for a number of useful purposes but this requires a shift in how teaching and learning is designed. Mobile devices have been shown to be problematic during a lecture as students are often distracted with social networking. While the natural reaction is to ban mobile devices, this is not the long-term solution. This situation reinforces the position that higher education must significantly rethink the value of the face-to-face classroom. For these devices to add value and be welcomed and used to enhance the quality of learning, the classroom must offer a more engaging learning experience. Consideration needs to be given to those educational activities that are best done in face-to-face or online environments.

The use of mobile technologies for educational purposes raises serious questions and has limitations with regard to their application. It is crucial that we understand the benefits of mobile devices for specific educational purposes. The advantage of online learning is that it makes possible more reflective comments. The question is whether this is facilitated when one is on the go? The point is that mobile communication may be great for personal communication and twittering, but it may not be best for serious academic discourse. This is also reflected in student and faculty concerns. It has been noted that "students are not necessarily ready to fully move into the mobile space for their coursework" (Brown & Diaz, 2010, p. 5) and faculty are not keen on learning to use yet another technology and having to adapt their curriculum accordingly. If we expect faculty to redesign their curriculum, the benefit must be transparent.

There remain many difficult questions with regard to using mobile devices in the classroom or for truly mobile learning. Educators need to proceed cautiously. The rationale for adopting mobile learning for academic purposes is not clear at this point. As noted previously, perhaps the real strength of highly mobile devices is to create social presence. This is an important element of collaborative approaches to learning, but may be best left to the informal social environment. While much of this is speculative at this point, new devices such as the iPad may well provide the means for e-learning to revolutionize higher education.

TEACHING AND TECHNOLOGY

Considering that this book is about understanding the application of e-learning in higher education, we cannot conclude this chapter without considering the influence that technology has had on learning. Knowledge development in this age is a "technologically aided activity" (Privateer, 1999, p. 62). It is imperative that those involved in higher education come to grips with the reality that technology is an increasingly important element of the educational environment and represents opportunities and constraints for interaction that can significantly influence the educational transaction. With a powerful technology and approach such as e-learning, its influence becomes more apparent, and it becomes crucial that we explore and consider that influence. The medium of communication does send an implicit message—and that message can enhance or diminish the intended educational experience.

Recently, researchers have come to question statements such as that by Clark (1983) who declared, "media are mere vehicles that deliver instruction, but do not influence student achievement any more than the truck that delivers our groceries causes changes in our nutrition" (p. 445). His argument was that it is the instructional design, mediated through learning activities, that affect learning outcomes (Clark, 1983, 1994). While the importance of instructional design cannot be denied, the issue is whether this generalization holds across various intended learning outcomes; or, to express it another way, whether characteristics of the technology of communication (specifically e-learning) can, in fact, have a significant influence on higher-order learning (Kozma, 1994). It has become less acceptable to accept the null hypothesis, as stated by Clark and others, that the means of communication has no effect on facilitating critical thinking and discourse and achieving higher-order learning outcomes.

The research into media use in educational contexts has consistently demonstrated no significant differences in learning outcomes when different delivery media were compared. However, it is important to note that much of this research did not control for the nature and quality of learning outcomes. In fact, most often the intended learning outcomes measured in these studies were the outcomes expected from low-level, information-assimilation educational experiences; that is, the re-statement of rote-learned facts and static information. But does the "no significant difference" generalization also hold when higher-order learning outcomes are intended, and where there is a shift in the mode of communication from oral to written language?

At least one pioneer in the use of written communication for educational purposes suggests that the null hypothesis does not hold. Feenberg (1999) states that writing is "not a poor substitute for physical presence and speech, but another fundamental medium of expression with its own properties and powers" (p. 345). The differences in the nature of spoken and written communication are, in fact, a key to understanding the effective use of computer-mediated communication and specifically e-learning. This echoes comments made by media researchers such as Olson (1994) who asserts that the written language is not just a pale shadow of the spoken language, but rather an independent entity with distinctive characteristics worthy of study in themselves. As Stein (1992) notes, a new, interdisciplinary "science of the text" is emerging. The issue of text versus speech was also raised as being of particular importance with regard to higher-order learning in Fabro & Garrison (1998). Add to this the recent research that indicates the superiority of blended learning over both face-to-face and online learning alone (Means, Toyama, Murphy, Bakia & Jones, 2009).

The critical point is that contextual variables (including specific technologies) do influence the nature and quality of learning outcomes. Contextual contingencies and learning activities must be congruent with intended and desired outcomes. What is learned is inseparable from how it is learned (Marton, 1988). This, of course, is a crucial realization when utilizing a technology that has unique communication characteristics. The method of transmission or communication is an important contextual influence. E-learning educators must be cognizant of the context they are creating from both a pedagogic and communications technology perspective.

CONCLUSION

Ultimately e-learning is not about technology, it is about flexibility, connectivity, and community. That said, the Internet and communications technologies have been the catalysts for the proliferation of e-learning. The challenge to the educational community to create collaborative constructivist learning designs has reached a new level of possibilities with the emergence of what has been labeled Web 2.0 tools. These tools have the enormous capability to bring together people to share and create knowledge. Brown & Adler (2008) properly shift the focus of Web 2.0 technologies to learning. They state, ". . . communities are harbingers of the emergence of a new form of technology-enhanced learning—learning 2.0—which goes beyond providing free access to traditional course materials and educational tools and creates a participatory architecture for supporting communities of learners" (p. 28).

Notwithstanding the large role played by communications technology, sound pedagogical ideas must be merged with the astounding capabilities of the new and emerging communication technologies. These tools must be used to approach educational ideals and meet the demands of a rapidly changing knowledge society. It is time to stop being seduced by the technology and trivial applications of that technology masquerading as an educational experience. We must not make the mistake that has too often happened in the past when educators adjust their pedagogy to accommodate the technology. We must do the sensible thing and ask what the technology can do to enhance the educational experience by making it more engaging and thought provoking. Higher education must critically evaluate what "role these innovations should play in effective teaching and learning" (Roblyer et al., 2010, p. 134).

Finally, the lesson to be drawn from the previous discussion is that "institutions should not think in terms of a single technological paradigm shift, but rather adopting a culture of continual change" (Ice, 2010, p. 158). The point is that not only is technology in a constant state of flux, the needs and challenges of higher education are also changing. The one thing that higher education has not been very good at is change. E-learning has been the main catalyst for change as it has offered solutions to the challenges of educational effectiveness and efficiency. When technological innovation is understood within the paradigm of e-learning, the focus is directed to using advances in information and communications technology to improving the educational process through the creation of a sense of community and collaboration. E-learning is the means to explore and understand how technology will evolve the teaching and learning transaction and enhance learning outcomes.

Chapter 8

Blended Learning

The greatest incursion of e-learning in higher education is through blended learning designs. However, as a result of the stealthy nature of blended learning, many educators are not fully aware of the influence that e-learning is having on higher education. Using online tools has become accepted and commonplace. Most courses in higher education have an e-learning presence in terms of online access to content, feedback, and discourse. This quiet revolution has been largely organic but we should not underestimate the transformational impact that blended learning represents. The only missing component to a more rapid transformation is proactive senior leadership in higher education strategically to recognize the need for more active learning experiences (see Chapter 11).

The challenge of engaging learners in higher education requires new ideas and approaches. It simply is not rational to continue to offer passive lectures and hope to increase active student engagement. Blended learning has the potential to serve the goal of higher-order thinking and learning. Moreover, the Community of Inquiry theoretical framework provides a coherent understanding of these cognitive goals and the essential conditions to achieve these goals. The CoI theoretical framework has been shown to be able to help us sort through the inherent complexities of a blended learning design (Garrison & Vaughan, 2008). The theoretical concepts and principles outlined in previous chapters apply equally well to a blended learning context. Keep in mind that e-learning was defined at the outset as consisting of both online and blended learning.

BLENDED LEARNING DESCRIBED

The core element in describing a blended learning design is the full integration of face-to-face and online activities. Simply adding optional or supplemental online activities to what is in essence a face-to-face learning experience does not meet the threshold of a blended learning design. The key is to integrate face-to-face oral and online written communication in such a way that the strengths of each are fused so that the result is greater than the best of the single constituting elements. For this reason, blended learning is defined here as "the organic integration of thoughtfully selected and complementary face-to-face and online approaches and technologies" (Garrison & Vaughan, 2008, p. 148).

When offering a definition of blended learning we need to be careful not to be too restrictive by setting rigid boundaries. If the intent is to rethink fundamentally how the course can best be delivered to meet the academic goals, and face-to-face and online activities are fully integrated, then it does not matter what exact percentage of time is spent in which mode of communication. The key is that the proportion of face-to-face and online experiences meets the needs for the educational purpose at hand. It is important that instructors have the opportunity to experiment with incorporating e-learning technology without worrying about labels and artificial standards. The great attribute of blended learning designs is the range of possibilities, to the point that virtually each course is unique in terms of the proportion and type of face-to-face and online learning experiences that are coherently employed.

An important value of blended learning is the fundamental rethinking of the educational approach. This is manifested in a restructuring of class contact hours. Fundamental rethinking is essential to not find ourselves in a position of simply layering on more activities and responsibilities without a consideration of what is important and reasonable from a time perspective. The goal is to design learning activities that are congruent with the educational aim. In its simplest form this means replacing passive listening with collaborative and reflective learning activities (such as case studies and projects) and, most importantly, it means increased interaction with the instructor. Blended learning can include the blending of individual and collaborative activities, modes of communication (verbal and written), and a range of face-to-face and online courses that constitute a blended program of studies. The possibilities are only limited by academic standards and educational imagination.

Scenarios

Considering the complexity of blended learning designs, to get a sense of the range of possibilities it is useful to provide some concrete examples. The most common challenge that a blended learning design is asked to address is the large enrolment course. The typical first-year undergraduate large enrolment lecture class can benefit substantially from a blended learning design. The goal is essentially to replace some or all of the lectures with engaging activities whether they are face-to-face or online. Face-to-face class time could be used more productively for team projects, labs or individual/small-group inter-action with the instructor. Online activities might include tutorials, discussion groups, or assessment. If some lectures are retained, they are used to introduce core ideas with the opportunity for students to question and interact in small groups. Personal response systems can be used effectively to engage students by having them report back individually or from a group perspective. More radical examples may include the creation of a drop-in lab with personal assistance where students work individually online receiving immediate feedback and assessment. This investment may be more appropriate for mega classes with hundreds of students each semester.

A blended learning approach can also be applied to medium-sized classes. These designs can be achieved with modest investment of resources. The goal is most likely more effective and efficient use of the instructor's time. While this scenario may require considerable investment at the front end of the redesign, the pay-off for the instructor is a much more engaging and enjoyable teaching experience. Examples may include pre-recording lectures and putting them online for students to view before class and then using class time for discussion and group tasks. A good example of this approach is in writing courses that shift from passive lectures to devoting greater time to the writing process itself (focus on applying knowledge). Face-to-face class time may be reduced and replaced with online or drop-in labs where academically appropriate. This may prove to be beneficial from the perspective of commuter students who may be afforded the convenience of reduced travel without compromising the quality of the educational experience.

More detailed examples of these and other blended learning designs can be found in Garrison & Vaughan (2008) as well as the National Center for Academic Transformation website (http://www.thencat.org/).

Online Blended Learning

There is another form of blending that combines asynchronous (written) and synchronous (verbal) online learning. Because this does not include face-to-face interaction, it is not technically blended learning as we have described it. However, it is an important form of e-learning and a form of blending worthy of consideration. Blending asynchronous and synchronous communication in an online environment has a significant advantage. In particular, the immediacy of synchronous verbal communication can enhance the development of a sense of community. The communication immediacy can be very effective in establishing social presence (trust, open communication, and group cohesion) and perceived learning (Baker, 2004; Swan & Richardson, 2003). This may be especially effective at the beginning of a course to create identification with the course, instructor, and fellow students. Verbal immediacy can also be a great benefit in an online environment when introducing a new topic in terms of efficiently focusing activities and addressing concerns.

Two leaders in this blending of asynchronous and synchronous communication in an online educational environment are Michael Power and

Norman Vaughan (http://www.bold-research.org/). These researchers have begun investigating what they call blended online learning designs (BOLD). They argue that there are important limits to asynchronous online learning. These quality concerns are associated with learner isolation that have been mitigated with online learning designs but have prevented a breakthrough in mainstream higher education (Power & Vaughan, 2010). What appears to be lacking is spontaneous dialogue and negotiation of meaning to counter the rigid structure of the asynchronous course package. Tentative early findings suggest there is more of an opportunity for dialogue and perhaps lower attrition. This latter suggestion is congruent with research noted previously with regard to a sense of community (cohesion) increasing persistence.

While this original research is in its infancy, it does suggest an opportunity to study the important properties of written and verbal communication in an e-learning context. This can only extend the influence and possibilities of e-learning.

WHY BLENDED LEARNING

The question for educators is why you would want to include online learning experiences in a campus-based learning environment. The educational rationale is the ability of a blended learning design to engage participants in critical reflection and discourse by creating a flexible and sustainable community of inquiry. Blended learning is about actively involving all participants in the educational enterprise. It means moving away from using scarce face-to-face time for information transmission. Blended learning designs can extend time and task that sustain a community of inquiry beyond the limited frame of the traditional face-to-face classroom. The range of design possibilities becomes apparent when we look at the combinations of face-to-face and online learning experiences and then imagine how they might be integrated for specific educational purposes.

Online learning provides a unique dimension to the face-to-face learning community that builds group cohesion. It encourages greater participation and thereby creates a greater sense of being part of the group. Asynchronous written communication is not only reflective but it is less intimidating and encourages intellectual risk taking. This freedom of expression then enhances the face-to-face session as students feel more comfortable to participate. In a counter-intuitive manner, online learning allows participants to reveal themselves in ways they might not in a face-to-face environment. They are less intimidated by the immediate presence of others in the group. There may also be increased opportunity for small group activities, and relationships have more time to build as communication is extended beyond the face-to-face classroom.

Notwithstanding the theoretical arguments for the power of blended learning and the significant shift in pedagogical thinking it encourages, there is growing evidence of its effectiveness. A recent meta-analysis study and review of e-learning by the U. S. Department of Education provided some interesting findings (Means, Toyama, Murphy, Bakia & Jones, 2009). The study initially identified 176 experimental or quasi-experimental studies of online learning from 1996 through to 2006. Most of these were from higher education and the main finding was:

> Learning outcomes for students who engaged in online learning exceeded those of students receiving face-to-face instruction . . .
>
> (Means et al., 2009, p. xiv)

The two significant influences on effectiveness were the use of blended approaches and time on task.

Specific to blending online and face to face, there were 99 studies that contrasted online or blended learning with face to face. Here it was found that:

> Instruction combining online and face-to-face elements had a larger advantage relative to purely face-to-face instruction than did purely online instruction.
>
> (Means et al., 2009, p. xv)

The findings strongly suggest a distinct advantage of blended learning over not only face-to-face but online learning as well. Insight into the reasons for this can be found in the fact that the second significant influence was time on task. It would seem that both online and blended learning provide increased time on task. Moreover, it is argued here that time on task is not only greatly extended in a blended learning design, but the quality of that time on task may be significantly greater when integrating the interactive strengths of verbal and written communication.

Finally, the study concluded that in recent studies, "[in] contrasting blends of online and face-to-face instruction with conventional face-to-face classes, blended instruction has been more effective, providing a rationale for the effort required to design and implement blended approaches" (Means et al., 2009, p. xvii). These findings are powerful statements about e-learning in general and blended learning in particular. They strongly support the theoretical arguments in support of blended learning. The conclusion is that online and blended learning (i.e., e-learning) appears to be an effective option in higher education. While caution must be exercised in generalizing these results, the findings are consistent with other research.

A series of studies using the CoI theoretical framework has provided some interesting insights into blended learning. One study focused on the perceptions of cognitive presence and the actual learning outcomes in an online and blended environment (Akyol & Garrison, in press a). While the actual grades were identical, it was found that "students in the blended course had higher perceptions of learning, satisfaction, cognitive presence, teaching presence and social presence" (Akyol & Garrison, in press a). Clearly there were perceived advantages to the blended learning approach. Considering that the grades were identical, one area that may be worth looking at would be persistence or completion rates. In this regard, it has been found that blended learning completion rates have been reported to be higher than online and many face-to-face courses (Dziuban, Hartman, Moskal, Sorg & Truman, 2004).

Another study in this series using the CoI theoretical framework focused on how blended learning supported the inquiry process. This was in partial response to earlier studies that appeared to show inquiry stalling at the exploration stage. In this study, Vaughan & Garrison (2005) found that the face-to-face environment was preferred for initiating discussions but the online environment was useful for expanding and sustaining the discussion. The results of this study suggest that online learning required participants to engage in greater integrative thinking (Vaughan & Garrison, 2005). This study also suggested that the resolution phase of inquiry (final solution) may well be best done in a face-to-face environment.

Along these same lines regarding the progression of inquiry, Akyol & Garrison (in press a) found increased frequency at the integration phase for blended compared to online learning. The explanation was an advantage of blended learning to use the face-to-face sessions to trigger the task and begin the exploration. While the nature of the task and teaching presence is still crucial for progression, it was concluded that blended learning may provide enhanced conditions for critical thinking (Akyol & Garrison, in press a). This is supported by other researchers in suggesting that the speed and energy of a face-to-face discussion at the exploration phase has been reported to benefit from a face-to-face environment (Meyer, 2003). Moreover, considering online discussions tend to be more reflective, focused, and thoughtful, this may well favor designing greater discourse at the integration phase.

However, as has been discussed in previous chapters, all elements of the community of inquiry must be working in concert if inquiry is to be effective in reaching intended learning outcomes. A research priority is to examine the three CoI presences simultaneously. In this regard, one study focused on all three CoI presences while exploring the differences between online and blended learning designs (Akyol, Garrison & Ozden, 2009). Differences in the social and cognitive presence dimensions were found between the online and blended design. In terms of social presence, group cohesion messages significantly favored the blended design. This is not surprising from a theoretical perspective as the blended students could make interpersonal and affective connections much more quickly. Online students apparently had to make more of an effort to create an affective presence. In this regard, class size was more of a problem for the online students in developing social presence. In short, developing social presence online took time.

With regard to teaching presence, the Akyol et al. (2009) study found that, because blended learning students could meet with the instructor face to face, blended students required less teaching presence and assumed more responsibility for facilitating and directing the online discussions. That is, there was a greater need for direct instruction in the online course. This perspective is also supported by the fact that students in the blended course had greater cohesion which may have supported increased collaboration and the ability of the students to assume teaching presence responsibilities. As noted in Chapter 7, teaching presence (design, facilitation, and direction) is of great importance in e-learning. Therefore, it is argued that the fact that students in a blended learning environment demonstrated increased teaching presence is a considerable advantage in achieving intended goals and in enhancing metacognitive awareness and abilities.

On another front, it has been recognized that there is a significant role adjustment to fully online learning (Cleveland-Innes, Garrison & Kinsell, 2007). The ease of adjustment to e-learning afforded by blended learning needs to be recognized as higher education transitions to more technologically mediated forms of communication. The first challenge is to ensure that the technology is congruent with the educational tasks. The real challenge, however, is creating and sustaining a community of inquiry where the presences are in dynamic balance. In this regard, Rovai & Jordan (2004) provided evidence that "blended courses produce a stronger sense of community among students than either traditional or fully online courses" (abstract, lines 5–6). It would seem that an effective community of inquiry may be best realized in a blended environment.

While we focused on the effectiveness of blended learning, there are considerable administrative efficiencies to be gained with its adoption. The efficiency of blended learning approaches is best evidenced in the work by the National Center for Academic Transformation (NCAT). The NCAT database of hundreds of course redesigns demonstrates conclusively that effectiveness and efficiencies are not mutually exclusive. The results of the initial course redesign projects, confirmed by numerous subsequent projects, found that institutions significantly reduced costs while increasing completion rates, student satisfaction, and improving or maintaining learning outcomes (Twigg, 2003). The ability to improve both effectiveness and efficiency should be seen as some kind of miracle for resource-challenged institutions of higher education. This is why it is only a matter of time before blended learning becomes the dominant approach to teaching and learning in higher education.

CONCLUSION

The limited number of blended learning research papers emphasizes the need for more studies into the pedagogical complexities of blended learning. Notwithstanding this limitation, there is a literature base in both face-to-face and online teaching and learning in higher education that can inform the study and practice of blended learning. Just as the CoI theoretical framework is a generic model, so too are most of the principles of teaching and learning in higher education. That said, there are challenges that must be resolved as we move forward with the adoption of blended learning designs. Students and instructors must be supported as they move from passive to collaborative forms of learning, both in terms of pedagogy and mastering the technology. Given the ever-present ability to engage in an e-learning environment, both students and faculty will need to learn to manage their time.

In closing, it should be emphasized that blended learning represents a significant conceptual and practical breakthrough in enhancing the quality of teaching and learning in higher education. It is inherently transformative and is quietly pervading higher education. Blended learning is a strategic solution to serious teaching and learning challenges. It is a thoughtful approach to an important problem. The great advantage of blended learning is that while it is transformative, it builds upon traditional ideals of communities of learners and familiar face-to-face learning. Notwithstanding the congruence of blended learning with traditional values of higher education and its capabilities to create and sustain communities of inquiry, blended learning initiatives are not always well received. Faculty need to be reminded of the traditional values of higher education associated with critical discourse in learning communities and be shown successful examples of blended learning designs that effectively and efficiently achieve these ideals.

A large part of the challenge in the adoption of blended learning in traditional institutions is related to change. Strong leadership will be evident in those institutions that effect this change successfully. It has been stated that the "impact of blended learning is potentially monumental—permanently changing how students interact with higher education . . ." (Laumakis, Graham & Dziuban, 2009, p. 86). While this will most likely represent evolutionary change, make no mistake, it will eventually transform higher education and build increasing credibility for all e-learning.

Chapter 9

Guidelines for Practice

Effective teaching requires more than a repertoire of techniques or recipes. The reality is that there is an abundance of "know how" books offering guidance on how to conduct an e-learning experience. These compendia of techniques provide little in the way of a coherent perspective or under-standing of the interplay between the collaborative (social) and constructivist (cognitive) dimensions of a teaching and learning transaction. Nor do they provide an appreciation of the elements and unique characteristics of the e-learning experience. The instructor, or if you wish, the facilitator, plays a key role throughout the e-learning experience—even when discourse and activities are largely regulated by the students. The instructor is an ever-present and key person, managing and monitoring the process. There is always a need for an instructor or facilitator to structure, shape, and assess the learning experience, if it is to be more than an informal or fortuitous learning experience.

In the first part of this book, the theoretical framework described the foun-dational concepts, principles, and organization of an e-learning experience. A pragmatic discussion of an e-learning experience is provided here. The discussion is embedded in the previous theoretical framework in order to provide a deeper understanding of the purposes and functions of various educational methods and techniques. There is an assumption as well with regard to the necessity to accommodate the inevitable changing cognitive and social dynamics of the CoI during an educational experience. Therefore, flexibility in terms of goals and methods must also be present as the educational progress develops. At the heart of this is the recognition of the relationship between learning activities and learning outcomes. Learning activities should be context dependent and congruent with intended out-comes.

LEARNING ACTIVITIES

Simple lists of learning activities or the latest trendy technique provide little rationale for selecting particular activities. The following classification (see Figure 9.1) identifies the four fundamental learning activities: listening, talking, reading, and writing. This figure helps us to understand the purposes and strengths of each learning activity. These activities are organized and understood from a cognitive or content perspective as well as from an organizational or transactional perspective.

For example, content has traditionally been assimilated largely through listening and reading. The counterpart to listening, that is, talking or verbal discourse, is too often severely limited in face-to-face environments with the result that less emphasis is implicitly placed on the collaborative construction of meaning and confirmation of understanding. Similarly, from the individual reflective perspective, we see a bias toward reading but fewer opportunities to rigorously bring ideas together coherently through the writing process. Educationally, we appear to be emphasizing information acquisition while limiting opportunities for critical discourse and higher-order knowledge construction.

From an e-learning point of view, the bias shifts to reading and writing activities, which, traditionally, are concomitant with private learning activities. This, of course, significantly changes in an e-learning context in that listening and talking are substituted for reading and writing. Reading and writing are both an individual and collaborative means of communication in an e-learning experience. Reading becomes both a means to acquire information as well as "listen" to the views of the instructor and students. Correspondingly, in an e-learning context, writing becomes the means to both construct meaning and communicate questions and ideas with members

	Exploratory (information acquisition)	Confirmatory (knowledge construction)
Group	LISTENING	TALKING
Individual	READING	WRITING

Figure 9.1 Learning Activities

Source Adapted from Garrison & Archer, 2000

of the learning community. With e-learning and computer conferencing, we listen by reading and talk by writing.

What place is there then for the traditional group activities of listening and talking? Are these activities simply abandoned in fully online e-learning experiences? If so, what do we lose educationally? It has been our experience, supported in the literature, that students very much value real-time verbal interaction. The question is how important are listening and talking activities and what is their function in a community of inquiry? As we have seen previously (Chapter 8), synchronous verbal communication can be blended with asynchronous communication in a fully online environment.

It would appear that verbal dialogue may have an advantage in the early, exploratory phases of practical inquiry. However, there is perhaps a stronger connection between verbal discourse and social presence. Experience has shown that e-learning students very much seek out other students, either face to face or by phone. Real-time, sustained verbal discourse is of considerable advantage in establishing social, cognitive, and teaching presence, particularly in the early phase of an educational experience. Notwithstanding this, having recognized the inherent differences in synchronous verbal communication and asynchronous text-based communication, the discussion here focuses on facilitating an asynchronous e-learning experience.

Before turning specifically to e-learning guidelines, we need to reiterate that teaching presence assumes an educational e-learning approach as neither a "sage on the stage" nor a "guide on the side." We believe that one is as biased as the other in approaching the design and delivery of an educational experience; however, considering the inherent complexity and challenges of an educational experience, there may be a place for either or both as the experience develops. An educational experience is properly composed of an instructor and student with a shared purpose. Contrary to what some contend (Collison, Elbaum, Haavind & Tinker, 2000), it is simply not true that the "guide on the side" is most appropriate for facilitating an e-learning experience. Considerable emphasis must be placed on teaching presence. This will become apparent as we explore the dimensions of teaching presence.

TEACHING–LEARNING GUIDELINES

We approach these guidelines from the perspective of teaching presence and its three sub-elements: design, facilitation, and direct instruction. Within each of the sub-elements of teaching presence we discuss issues of social and cognitive presence that the teaching function must address. Teaching presence encompasses more than the exchange of messages. In addition to the facilitation of critical discourse, it includes readings, exercises, Web explorations, blogs or wikis, and collaborative projects, to name a few. The first challenge is to consider which activities to include and how they will be integrated into a meaningful educational experience. Design is the first element of teaching presence and must be approached by concurrently considering both social and cognitive presence issues.

Design and Organization

To begin with, we must appreciate that the roles of instructor and student in an e-learning transaction are both congruent with, and different from, their roles in a traditional face-to-face classroom experience. That is, as discussed in Chapter 2, the essential elements in approaching an educational experience in a collaborative constructivist manner remain inviolable. At the same time, in terms of asynchronous text-based communication and the accessibility to resources, e-learning represents a paradigm shift in how the teaching and learning transaction plays out. It is to these issues and their practical implications that we turn our attention.

Adjustment to an e-learning context includes the need to plan for both social and cognitive impacts. Roles for all participants, including instructors and students, will require significant adjustment. This is particularly true for first-time online students who have to adjust to written communication and participation in a community of inquiry. While students need to adapt to a more collaborative approach, instructors may have a greater challenge in learning how to balance facilitation and direction to achieve a deep and meaningful level of interaction. Identifying with and engaging in an online community of learners is unlike most higher education classrooms. Some general role-adjustment design considerations are to make explicit adjustment challenges, provide technology support, and ensure greater instructor involvement at the beginning (Cleveland-Innes, Garrison & Kinsell, 2007). More specific adjustments are discussed below.

The process of planning a quality e-learning experience is very likely to be more complex and time consuming than planning a conventional classroom experience. Thinking through the structure, process, and evaluation aspects of an e-learning course raises special challenges. The introduction and orientation of an e-learning experience will greatly influence sustained motivation and must, therefore, be carefully considered. These challenges also present opportunities to do things better educationally through more transparent teaching presence and modeling. Teaching presence must be an integral aspect of a community of inquiry and not an external authority function. To ensure a true inquiry-based approach, teaching presence responsibilities must be shared by all participants to greater and lesser degrees as the course of studies progress. For this reason, much of the success of the e-learning experience will depend on design and organization.

It is important to appreciate that, in a collaborative constructivist approach, design is not a rigid template that is imposed on the learning situation. The design must be inherently flexible and adaptable to unpredictable and individual learning needs as they arise. Design and redesign continue throughout the educational experience as collaboration and shared control introduce a creative element of uncertainty. This constructivist freedom with an educational purpose takes advantage of the great strength of e-learning and outlines a major advantage over conventional passive face-to-face approaches or prescriptive, self-instructional course packages characteristic of traditional distance education. Curricula must be relatively open and all are active participants, not spectators. Moreover, students must have an appropriate degree of control over the monitoring and regulation of their activities and learning. Responsibility and control must naturally evolve and grow as the learner progresses socially and cognitively. This developmental theme is reflected in each of the subsequent sections on the design of social and cognitive presence. This helps us understand what kinds of activities and support are needed in progressive phases of learning.

From a design and organizational perspective, specific guidelines and suggestions for practice include:

1 establishing curriculum;
2 identifying resources;
3 defining clear expectations and goals (process and content);
4 addressing technological concerns;
5 structuring activities (collaborative and individual);
6 setting time-frames;
7 devising assessment processes and instruments.

These must be considered in depth both before and during the e-learning experience. During the design phase instructors must do their best to provide reasonable structure (goals, expectations) and anticipate as best they can the evolving needs of the students.

While specific design suggestions will follow, a comment about addressing technological concerns is appropriate here. It is easy to say that technology should be transparent (so that users are not consciously aware of the technology), but this is an ideal, predicated on training and support. The transparency issue is compounded by the constant introduction of new media and standards. It may be a special challenge to provide technology training and support for students at a distance. (It should be noted that technology and associated training is important but exogenous to the core of the CoI theoretical framework.) While instructor in-service in the use of technology can often be done in face-to-face seminars and workshops, consideration should be given to online support. For students, special efforts may be needed to have them become comfortable with the technology. Experience has shown that technology training will invariably require more time than is initially estimated. Greatest success is achieved where training is offered in stages and where new training is applied immediately.

Social Presence

Because fully online e-learning can be accompanied by a sense of isolation, one of the first and most important challenges for the teacher is to establish social presence. It is crucial that each student feels welcomed and is given the reassurance that they are part of a community of learners. This sense of belonging and security facilitates open communication and creates group cohesion. Social presence is essential in a collaborative learning experience and is an important element in establishing cognitive presence.

From a social presence perspective it is helpful to understand the developmental dynamics of groups. Even though groups do vary considerably in their cohesiveness and evolution, some insight into group dynamics can be useful in anticipating social conflicts or reduced motivation. There are several group development theories that essentially confirm that groups evolve in a relatively systematic manner (Pratt, 1981). This fact has been confirmed by the study of Akyol & Garrison (2008) discussed previously in Chapter 6.

In the initial phase, students must feel included if they are to form a cohesive community of inquiry. In the middle, or productive phase, there will inevitably be conflicts and the need for resolution. It is difficult to predict when, and to what degree, conflict will manifest itself. One should be aware of this difficulty because the process might not surface in an overt and obvious way, but may still have a detrimental effect on open communication and group cohesion. If students are to take control and responsibility for their learning, then instructors must expect challenges and conflict. The key is to address these conflicts constructively with negotiation and respect. As groups bond, endings become important. Preparation for transition and emotional closure are issues that should be addressed (Pratt, 1981). Consideration of these dynamics provides the climate to establish cognitive presence.

Some conflict is inevitable and is not unhealthy if skepticism and critical reflection are to be encouraged. The goal is to create trust but not discourage respectful dissent or criticism. Here, teachers can model the appropriate behavior by opening themselves to challenges from students. Paralleling the characteristics of reflection and dialogue inherent in asynchronous e-learning, students must be separate but part of the community. That is, they must be allowed and encouraged to maintain cognitive independence to construct meaning while contributing to mutual understanding.

Preparation for the first session is important in any educational experience, but crucial in an e-learning context. In establishing social presence, paradoxically, the vehicle should be substantive educational concerns and issues. Certainly, special efforts must be made to allow participants to introduce themselves, but the first session should not be just a social event. It must be remembered that the purpose of establishing social presence is to support and enhance a purposeful critical community of inquiry. Through the use of chat rooms, collaborative assignments, and discourse associated with subject-related critical inquiry, students will gain trust and develop relationships over time. Once established, social presence will recede to the background as academic challenges grow.

While student motivation may initially be high, sustaining this motivation throughout the course of studies will, to a considerable extent, be a function of cohesion and collaboration. Consideration must be given to anticipating how to involve reluctant students as well as focus or limit contributions from overenthusiastic participants. Not all students will feel comfortable in an e-learning environment and they will need to know the rules and etiquette. Here, clear expectations as to the length and frequency of contributions should be provided before the course begins. Although not all students need to participate at the same frequency as their peers, they should be made aware to stay in touch on a regular basis. Accommodation must be made for individual differences and this is why decisions regarding assigning grades based upon participation need to be made with care.

The great challenge for teachers in establishing social presence is setting the right tone at the right time. The right tone may range from nurturing and emotional support to questioning and analytical responses. The tone of the conversation should correspond with cognitive presence issues and goals. At times the instructor may be a guide on the side (i.e., facilitator) and at times a sage on the stage (i.e., direct instruction)—or, at other times, something in between in the role of an active moderator. All these roles require teaching presence with a specific educational goal in mind.

The first sub-element of teaching presence, design and organization, should build a special presence that establishes:

1   a feeling of trust and being welcomed;
2   a sense of belonging to a critical community;
3   a sense of control;
4   a sense of accomplishment;
5   a willingness to engage in discourse;
6   a conversational tone; and
7   a questioning attitude.

Suggested activities to establish social presence to be considered at the design stage might include:

1   introductory email from instructor, including short bio;
2   student web pages sharing a short bio and expectations;
3   discuss and negotiate expectations in small groups;

4   informal coffee shop discussion board;
5   netiquette and code of conduct.

Cognitive Presence

Ultimately the purpose of any educational experience is learning; but not just indiscriminate or fortuitous learning. The premise of this book is that e-learning is more than the undirected, unreflective exchange of opinions. Higher education places value on reflective thinking and higher-order learning outcomes. The critical thinking process required to achieve these outcomes necessitates complex and sustained communication between and among the instructor and students. Analysis and acceptance of the dialogic writing process in an e-learning environment is essential.

To provide insight specific to the learning process, we have focused on a community of inquiry and the cognitive processes associated with the model of practical inquiry. Cognitive presence is created directly through critical reflection and dialogue described by the Practical Inquiry (PI) model. The four phases of PI associated with cognitive presence are:

1   a triggering event and sense of puzzlement or dissonance;
2   exploring an issue or problem through gathering and exchanging relevant information;
3   integrating or making sense of this information by connecting the ideas in a meaningful way; and
4   resolving the issue by applying and testing the ideas either directly or vicariously.

Although students are capable of progressing through these phases, this will not likely happen without some guidance and this must be considered when designing and organizing an educational experience. The transformation from the triggering and exploring stages to the integration and resolution stages of inquiry will depend on the nature of the assignment. Teaching presence is essential to ensure movement to the integration and resolution phase. The division of the plenary group into smaller groups for discussion can be very beneficial for establishing cognitive and social presence.

Associated with teaching presence is the responsibility to design a variety of appropriate learning activities congruent with the cognitive task. In designing an effective educational experience, particular consideration should be given to the use and development of case-based studies. Case studies focus discussion from a real-world perspective that students can relate to. They can utilize small and large group discussions, encourage students to take responsibility for extracting meaning, and provide opportunities for students to moderate discussions. Used in these ways, case-based studies can provide the perfect context for the teacher to explore an important issue, introduce an organizing concept (big idea), and to reach resolution.

From a cognitive presence design perspective, two issues (content and assessment) stand out. First, if higher-order learning outcomes are valued, then students must not be overloaded with excess content. The great risk in too much content is that, directly or indirectly, it sends the message that the goal is to assimilate information. Students must have time to reflect, make sense of the content, and share understanding with participants. Cognitive tasks will change, but the process of iterating between reflection and discourse is constant. With virtually unlimited access to information in e-learning, considerable thought needs to be given to organizing information so students do not get lost in the details.

Second, cognitive presence will be strongly influenced by assessment and grading. Simply put, assessment must be congruent with intended learning outcomes. If the educational goals are higher-order learning outcomes, then assignments must be congruent with, and tests must assess, this level of learning. It is not good enough to emphasize critical discourse when students will be tested and graded on information recall. The quality of discourse and participation will drop rapidly and students will devote their limited time to activities that are rewarded—assimilation of information. This incongruence between activity and assessment creates frustration for all and limits the potential of e-learning. We do not need the power of e-learning to support a collaborative constructivist educational experience if all we intend to do is transmit information and assess recall.

Asynchronous communication inherently provides for both reflection (constructivism) and discourse (collaboration). The challenge for the teacher is to know when to emphasize one or the other. At the beginning of a learning experience, considerable structure and support is required to establish cognitive presence. Beyond clear content goals, it may be extremely advantageous to provide a metacognitive map of the PI model so students have an awareness of their responsibilities in constructing meaning and understand the progression of their learning activities and tasks. One technique that might be considered is to have students label their discussion contributions according to the phase of inquiry. This will create both knowledge and regulation of the inquiry process. Students need to understand that greater cognitive presence (i.e., responsibility) will be expected as the course progresses.

Cognitive presence issues associated with design and organization include:

1 consideration of assessment of cognitive development and knowledge at the entry level;
2 organization and limitation of curriculum;
3 selection of appropriate learning activities;
4 provision of time for reflection;
5 integration of small discussion groups and sessions;

6 provision of opportunities to model and reflect upon the critical thinking process;

7 design of higher-order learning assessment rubrics.

Suggested activities to establish cognitive presence to be considered at the design stage might include:

1 plan for question-driven and problem-based learning activities;

2 use small breakout groups;

3 allow time to engage and complete the assignment;

4 have students share a powerful learning experience and discuss why it was eventful;

5 a WebQuest collaboratively to search, analyze, and synthesize information from the internet.

Facilitating Discourse

Discourse goes to the core of the e-learning experience. Interaction and discourse are the strengths of e-learning and are the essence of a community of inquiry educational experience. Facilitation is a key responsibility in creating and managing educationally worthwhile discourse. Facilitating discourse for the purpose of constructing meaning and confirming understanding requires a delicate balance between too little and too much intervention. Facilitating discourse first requires a climate that will precipitate participation and reflective discussion.

Social Presence

Education by definition is socially situated. The need for social presence is derivative of this reality. Social presence is essential to creating a community of inquiry central to a higher education learning experience. Education is more than transmitting and assimilating content. It is about reflecting on, questioning, analyzing, and testing ideas. These basic activities do not thrive in a group without personal affiliation or where expression is not open and relatively risk free. A sense of isolation or of not being connected will not encourage or support critical inquiry, nor will it engender motivation resulting from a shared experience that provides acknowledgement and a sense of accomplishment. Without these affective and interpersonal elements, engaging students and realizing cognitive attitudes and skills to sustain learning are less than certain.

It is very difficult to discuss social presence in the absence of cognitive presence. For example, responding to an individual's message, or expressing agreement, adds to both social and cognitive presence. Cognitive interaction, so essential to a collaborative constructivist educational experience, is predicated on, and sustained by, the social relationships and cohesion of the group. Practical inquiry is an inseparable iteration between reflection and discourse; between private and public worlds. For this reason, separation of social and cognitive presence is not sustained in practice. Therefore, while we focus first on social presence guidelines and suggestions, cognitive presence issues are ever present.

In addition to having students post short bios (preferably in a chat room), a good start to an e-learning course is to form the students into small groups and ask each group to identify questions they may have about content and process expectations. These issues can then be brought to the class as a whole. This not only creates an opportunity for the instructor to set the right tone for critical inquiry by clarifying process concerns and negotiating course expectations, but it allows students to become familiar with other students and the technology. Through open communication instructors can reveal their thought processes, thereby enhancing metacognitive awareness and making themselves personally more accessible to students. Although the instructor must remain professional, revealing aspects of one's academic qualifications and, to some extent, personal interests can contribute to a welcoming and more relaxed environment. Students must feel secure but discussion should be purposeful and cognitively challenging. For this reason, it needs to be made clear that purely social or personal exchanges are welcomed but are best conducted in a chat room or coffee house.

Suggestions to facilitate social presence and establish a community of inquiry are:

1 Acknowledge and welcome participants as they enter a discussion.
2 Be encouraging and supportive while directing discussion.
3 Project your personality as a teacher and allow students to get to know you as a person to the degree appropriate for the context.
4 Suggest that students log on at least three times per week.
5 Encourage students to acknowledge individuals when responding to specific contributions.
6 Laud contributions when appropriate.
7 Be conversational and not too formal in communications.
8 Encourage "lurkers" to participate.
9 Express feelings but avoid flaming.
10 Be cautious using humor, at least until familiarity is achieved.
11 Encourage students to inform the teacher by e-mail of tensions or anxiety.

Cognitive Presence

Cognitive presence goes to the heart of an educational experience. That is, creating and sustaining a community of inquiry where students are engaged in a collaborative and reflective process which includes understanding an issue or problem, searching for relevant information, connecting and integrating information, and actively confirming the understanding. The focus here is managing the process and monitoring the depth of understanding. This involves facilitating and focusing the discourse, providing appropriate insights and information when needed, and seeking common understanding or insight.

The first challenge from a community of inquiry perspective is getting the attention of the students and engaging them in meaningful discussions. Depending on the learning objective and the subject matter, there are typically two ways to approach this. The first approach is to provide one or two intriguing questions along with some associated readings or a case study. The goal is to have the students define the key question or issue, find the relevant information, suggest some meaningful connection or order, and agree on a resolution. Students may be expected to explore the Web for additional relevant information that can be reported on and bookmarked for future reference. Here, the instructor is very much a moderator and guide. This approach is inductive, with the emphasis on creating order. The second approach is more deductive in nature and is more appropriate with well-ordered or defined subject matter. The goal of this approach is to provide a model or framework (perhaps competing models) then challenge the students to gain some depth of understanding by testing applications in contexts familiar to them.

The core element and task, however, is facilitating (initiating, sustaining, and summarizing) stimulating and meaningful discourse where students actively participate, critically challenge arguments, and take responsibility for making sense of the course content. To lecture (i.e., deliver content) online is to negate the power and capability of e-learning and, most detrimentally, to turn students into passive receivers of information. Critical inquiry is content specific and needs to be led by a facilitator with content as well as context (pedagogical) expertise. That is, they must know their subject, but they must also have pedagogical expertise and know-how to moderate critical discourse in a largely text-based asynchronous learning environment. Facilitating deep understanding necessitates questioning, searching for key concepts, making connections, injecting new ideas or concepts, constructing frameworks, diagnosing misconceptions, and reviewing and summarizing. This requires knowing when to give and take control, when to encourage student input, and when to inform.

Particular care must be exercised when moving the discourse to the latter phases of inquiry. Due to tasks or assignments that do not require resolution and a too passive facilitation approach, many e-learning educational experiences stall on the exploration phase and students are left to their own devices to create some order and resolve the dilemma—or not. Here the facilitator must have it clearly in mind that there will be resolution. This resolution may be predictable or it may not, depending on how well defined the subject matter or task is. In any case, there must be a relentless shaping of the discourse through the phases of inquiry. That does not mean that it is a simple linear process or that all phases are of equal importance. In practice, there will be iteration between and among phases and more time will be spent on some phases than others. For example, in less well-defined subject areas, the focus may be on exploration and integration. In well-defined subject areas, the focus may be largely on resolution and finding solutions to specific problems.

One constant in this process is the need for discourse to stimulate and guide reflection. This is often best done in smaller groups (not a constraint in an e-learning context). These discussions should be private, unless the facilitator is invited in. Each group would be expected to assume responsibility for teaching presence and be required to report back to the full class. It is here that students are free to share their learning experiences and attempts to construct meaning. They will also learn how to facilitate critical discourse and direct the progress of the group. Small-group discussion can be used in all phases of inquiry to foster increased participation, focus on fewer discussion threads, and develop responsibility to construct meaning. However, it should be noted that large or whole-class discussion sessions have the advantage of more ideas and a diversity of viewpoints (McCarthy, Smith & DeLuca, 2010).

As noted, small groups provide an opportunity to allow the students to moderate discussions. Student moderation can attenuate the authoritative influence of an instructor and encourage freer discussion. However, student-moderated discussions may lack a needed degree of content expertise and, as a result, may not have the same ability to weave responses, add important information, and encourage critically reflective comments. Moderation can be a very valuable experience for students but they should have some guidance and oversight from the teacher (Rourke & Anderson, 2002). Students can be resentful if they feel abandoned by the instructor.

Encouraging students to monitor and regulate their learning is the means of increasing metacognitive awareness. Considerable attention should be directed to increasing metacognitive awareness to give students a better understanding of critical thinking and the inquiry process. Metacognitive awareness will provide a cognitive map of inquiry and the complexities of critical discourse. The PI model can be a guide for the teacher and students in progressing through the phases of critical thinking and discourse. Consideration should be given to introducing the CoI theoretical framework and PI model before engaging in discourse. This may well strongly shape the nature and quality of contributions.

If students are to become lifelong learners, then they must be cognizant of the purpose and process of learning activities. Students should be provided opportunities to monitor and regulate their activities and responses if we are to encourage them to judge the success of their learning strategies and tactics. That is, students need to be aware of their thinking in order to regulate that thinking. This awareness will go a long way to move e-learning discussion beyond the early exploratory phase and on to the integration and application of new ideas and concepts.

A great technique to have students increase their metacognitive awareness, knowledge, monitoring and regulating skills, is to encourage them to think about their online contributions by having them label their responses and keep track of other discussion responses (Pawan, Paulus, Yalcin & Chang, 2003). Within the context of the CoI theoretical framework and the PI model, this would mean labeling responses according to each of the phases of inquiry. This has been shown to produce a higher level of cognitive processing (Valcke et al., 2009). Another practical advantage of metacognitive awareness would be to make students aware that they are not progressing in a timely manner and may be stalling on one of the phases of inquiry.

Cognitive presence issues associated with facilitating discourse can be summarized as:

1 Focus discussion on key issues.
2 Provide stimulating questions.
3 Identify puzzling issues arising from responses.
4 Challenge ideas and precipitate reflection.
5 Moderate but do not overly direct discussion.
6 Test ideas theoretically or vicariously through application.
7 Move on when discussion ebbs or has served its purpose.
8 Facilitate metacognitive awareness by having students label the nature of their comments in terms of the phases of the PI model.

Direct Instruction

The element of direct instruction is what clearly moves e-learning into an educational experience. It is the responsibility of the instructor to provide intellectual and pedagogic leadership. In higher education, the instructor is expected to set the intellectual climate, design the curriculum, model the characteristics of an inquisitive scholar, and initiate students into the nuances of the subject. Challenges will require direct intervention but with openness and integrity such that the student understands and is a participant in the transaction. Scaffolding (i.e., temporary support to develop higher cognitive skills) is an important component of most socially shared (i.e., collaborative constructivist) cognitive models of learning. This is not accomplished with a laissez-faire or passive collective approach.

Social Presence

While on the surface it might seem that direct instruction would diminish social presence, it may well have just the opposite effect. First, let us reiterate that cognitive and social presence issues are interdependent. Regardless of the cognitive challenges facing instructors and students, education is a collaborative and, therefore, social institution. Second, direct instruction can raise important social presence considerations, demonstrating respect and relating to individuals or the group in a non-threatening way. Students very much value teaching presence but they must also be comfortable questioning or even challenging direct instruction.

Another area justifying direct intervention is when a few students dominate the discussion or intimidate others and prevent them from joining in. Here, direct instruction is required to encourage these students to listen to others and reflect upon larger chunks of the discourse. Similarly in a highly interactive e-learning environment conflict may arise that needs to be managed. While intervention may be required if conflict interferes with class dynamics, in general students should be left to their own devices for minor squabbles. Over time, it can be expected that students will become increasingly socially and cognitively responsible. However, a single student can be disruptive to the point that open communication and discourse is seriously compromised. For the sake of group cohesion, disruptive individuals should be confronted directly through personal communication.

Social presence issues associated with direct instruction are consistent with previous issues but must be approached with particular care as the comments are specific and often directed to individuals. Some suggestions are:

1   Shape discussion but don't dominate.
2   Provide feedback with respect.
3   Be constructive with corrective comments.
4   Be open to negotiation and providing reasons.
5   Deal with conflict quickly and privately.

Cognitive Presence

The virtual nature of an e-learning experience only enhances the need for teaching presence. Students need feedback and direction for cognitive reasons or because of time constraints and the need to expedite the educational process. As a subject matter expert, explaining questions or clarifying misconceptions is not only constructive but an important teaching-presence responsibility. Following from this, we strongly believe that a knowledgeable instructor has a responsibility to either frame the content or direct attention to specific concepts that form the basis of an organizing framework. In this way, students have, or can construct, the schema that goes beyond isolated facts and provides the foundation to facilitate continuous knowledge development. Regardless, this will necessitate appropriate intervention. The instructor's role goes beyond a neutral weaving of participants' contributions.

Direct instruction should be approached with the intent of taking learners to higher levels of cognitive development than they might have otherwise reached if they had operated independently. This means implementing, monitoring, and ending a range of learning activities and tasks that have specific learning objectives in mind. This requires direct instruction and solicitation of formative feedback. Deep and meaningful learning depends on diagnosing misconceptions, and depends on other forms of formative evaluation that the instructor can use to intervene directly. These are important forms of teaching presence.

On the other hand, lecturing and dictating values and viewpoints is a misuse of the technology and perhaps of the educational process. Too much direct instruction will assuredly reduce interaction and limit critical reflection to the detriment of higher-order learning experiences. Students must have the opportunity to contribute and develop their ideas. This requires a delicate balance where the situation may call for instructor participation, while at other times the discussion may need direction or to be brought to a close. Direct instruction most often obliges students to look deeper into a topic.

Summarizing discourse segments at the end of a course is also a crucial direct intervention. At these points it is often appropriate to extract key concepts and direct students to further learning challenges. This is important from both a cognitive and social presence perspective. Cognitively, it can create a sense of accomplishment and provide an evaluation of the course. Socially, it is an opportunity to have some closure and bid others farewell.

Cognitive presence issues associated with direct instruction can be summarized as:

1 Offer alternative ideas and perspectives for analysis and discussion.
2 Respond directly to and elaborate on inquiries for all to absorb.
3 Acknowledge uncertainty where it exists.
4 Make connections among ideas.
5 Collaboratively construct knowledge structures.
6 Summarize discussion and move on.
7 Provide closure and foreshadow further study.

CONCLUSION

The focus of this chapter has been on practical aspects of teaching presence. In each of the three teaching presence sub-elements (design, facilitation, and direct instruction), relevant issues of social and cognitive presence were discussed and guidelines provided. However, e-learning is a fast-moving area of study and practice. For this reason, instructors need to be teaching scholars if they are to remain current. This represents a considerable challenge when combined with the additional workload of designing and delivering an e-learning educational experience. To compound the challenge, there are enormous administrative responsibilities and organizational issues that need also to be considered.

Chapter 10

Assessment and Evaluation

In this chapter, the critical role of assessment and evaluation in ensuring a quality e-learning experience is examined. Although the terms assessment and evaluation have occasionally been used synonymously, we differentiate between the two terms. Assessment is used, in this text, to refer to its role in determining students' learning processes and outcomes. Such assessment is, by necessity, multifaceted and can include: acquisition of skills and behavioral competencies; competency in applying cognitive skills, including capacity to apply critical and creative solutions to complex problems; and attitudinal demeanor, including capacity to be critical, supportive, or enthusiastic as required in the context of a community of inquiry. Generally, assessment occurs throughout the course, thereby providing formative feedback to students, and at the completion of the course providing summative information on learning accomplishments to both student and instructor.

On the other hand, evaluation is used to refer to the act of comparing a unit, course, or program against some set of performance or outcome criteria. These criteria are often set by external agents or organizations, but the interests of the teacher and students are also driving forces within evaluation policies. Comprehensive evaluation includes measures of learning, satisfaction, costing and cost benefits, and other criteria for program success as defined by any or all relevant stakeholders or participants.

ASSESSING E-LEARNING

The importance of assessment in an educational experience cannot be overestimated. As Rowntree (1977) states, "If we wish to discover the truth about an educational system, we must look into its assessment procedures" (p. 1). This is one of the great truths and constants of an educational transaction. There is general consensus that assessment fundamentally shapes learning, particularly if we hope to approach learning in a deep and meaningful manner (Garrison & Archer, 2000). When it comes to the pedagogical importance and influence of assessment in an educational experience, e-learning is not exempt.

The focus of the discussion about e-learning here is from an educational perspective and, therefore, much of the theory and practice of a quality educational experience that has been developed for campus-based education has direct relevance in designing assessment for e-learning. However, it is also true that the context within which education is practiced effects design and delivery. Assessment in an e-learning context is complicated by many factors, including: the effects of the communication media; the lack of physical proximity and body language used for feedback in classrooms; the limited instructor supervision over the learning process; the difficulty of authentication and cheating on exams in distributed contexts; and the likely reduction of informal, after-class interaction.

Assessment is directly linked to effective teaching and learning by revealing understanding and achievement. For assessment to be successful it must first be congruent with intended learning outcomes. For example, if the goal is to realize deep understanding of concepts and develop critical thinking abilities, the focus of assessment must be understanding and thinking—not the recall of fragmented bits of information. Therefore, assessment should diagnose misconceptions during the learning process and assess the quality of intended learning outcomes. This form of in-depth assessment is not for the faint of heart in any educational experience and it is no less challenging in an e-learning environment. However, the challenges can be mitigated through the effective use of the interactive and collaborative characteristics of e-learning and the use of activities and assessment consistent with this potential for collaboration.

Functions of Assessment

Notwithstanding the challenges of assessment in an e-learning context, considering the properties and potential of e-learning, the focus needs to be on assessing collaborative learning. Unfortunately, the tradition of higher education is that assessment is focused on content assimilation and other instructor-centered techniques. If we are to capitalize on the collaborative potential of e-learning we need to include techniques that recognize and reward collaborative learning. If collaborative learning is not valued and reflected through assessment processes, authentic participation and higher-order learning will be compromised. Considering the strength of e-learning in support of collaborative constructivist/reflective learning, this "requires a radical rethinking of assessment methodologies" (Swan, Shen & Hiltz, 2006, p. 46).

Collaborative learning is more than a means to an end in terms of content acquisition. It is the means to deep understanding and metacognitive aware-ness that facilitates continuous learning. For this reason it is important to have at least some formative feedback and assessment on the nature and quality of the collaborative process. Students should be asked to comment on what went well and what did not in terms of the collaborative transaction. However, assessing collaborative learning should not be done at the expense of assessing individual learning. Assessing collaborative and individual learning reflects the shared and private worlds inherent in practical inquiry. A means must be found to provide a grade for both collaborative and individual accomplishments. Consideration must be given to assessing collaborative assignments. One way to do this is for the group to submit the completed comprehensive assignment and have each participant submit their particular contribution to the collaborative project. Other means are self-assessment, peer assessment, and group presentations.

The CoI theoretical framework speaks to the educational transaction and the need to provide feedback on a continuous basis. Formative assessment provides feedback to students on their progress toward attaining educational goals and objectives. Formative assessment motivates and guides students in an effective and efficient manner. Students are more likely to persevere when their purposeful activities are acknowledged and rewarded. Thus, formative assessment serves the fundamentally important role of providing feedback to students on their often considerable and challenging collaborative and reflective learning efforts.

Assessment also plays a critical function by providing external benchmarks that can be internalized. Since knowledge is both externally and internally defined, assessment provides an integrating mechanism whereby external measures of learning accomplishments are matched with a personal understanding of the learning process (metacognition). Such metacognitive awareness enhances learner responsibility and control and better equips students for continuous learning. Learners are also motivated by assessment techniques. Effective instructors use assessment techniques strategically to motivate learners to engage successfully in productive learning activities. Successful learners most often rely on assessment deadlines and activities both to pace and direct their learning efforts.

Having articulated the value of assessment in an educational learning experience, we now turn the discussion to the means by which assessment is best used in an e-learning context.

Assessing Participation

Assessment must be linked to, and be congruent with, course objectives and activities if it is to be useful in achieving intended outcomes. Many of us have had the experience of devising enrichment or suggested activities for students, only to realize that most students are too instrumentally focused and too busy with other commitments to undertake many un-credited optional tasks. However, throughout this book we have been arguing for the integration of cognitive, social, and teaching presence through participation in e-learning communities of inquiry—mostly supported through asynchronous text interaction. Therefore, educational tasks and activities should be core to outcome expectations and be assessed accordingly. Given the necessity to relate effort to reward, we must confront the question of how best to assess and reward student participation in e-learning conferences or discussion boards—activities central to a community of inquiry.

It is clear that students must perceive participation in online discussions as a core component of the program of studies. Thus, assessment activities must be integrated within e-learning activities. However, teachers must also be careful not to structure the discourse overly through excessive assessment and personal intervention. The social presence of the e-learning environment must be welcoming and positive enough that students willingly respond and support each other in cognitive growth. On the other hand, omnipresent assessment may lead students to conclude that the discussion is a "teacher tool" and not one over which they have any control or ability to modify to meet their individual and group educational needs. Students should have some input into assessment if they are to be encouraged to be self-directed and have metacognitive awareness.

Students perceive that their participation and resulting learning is related to the grades assigned for participation by the instructor. Such reward for participation is unlike most classroom education, where it is common not to provide grades for attendance and participation. Jiang & Ting (2000), in their report on college students studying via networked learning, found that students' perceived learning was significantly correlated to the percentage of grade weight assigned to participation and their resulting participation in discussion. Thus, it is important for teachers to value students' participation both informally, through frequent interaction among themselves, and formally, through feedback and assessment.

In an e-learning community of inquiry approach, discourse is the prime component of the learning process. Palloff & Pratt (2005) argue that given this emphasis on the process of learning, participation in the process must be assessed and appropriately rewarded. Most students have competition for their time and are unlikely to participate in activities that are marginal or viewed as supplemental to the course goals and grading assessment. For this reason, it is crucially important that students be provided with guidelines for arguing a position and grading rubrics that state assessment criteria and percentage of final grade for participation. Research has shown that effective discussion is associated with assessment and, more specifically, there is evidence to suggest that discussions shaped by assessment rubrics show "more posts, more threads, and a greater depth than . . . discussions in the classes given no discussion criteria" (Swan, Schenker, Arnold & Kuo, 2007, p. 78).

The following rubric, Figure 10.1, was designed to assess an online discussion moderated by a student. The goal was to identify the key components or responsibilities for moderating the discussion and then to define the quality characteristics or performance levels associated with each component. This rubric was created by a colleague of mine, Norm Vaughan, when we co-taught a blended course on the topic of blended learning. Another rubric that might be developed would be to assess the quality of participation according to the phases of the Practical Inquiry model. For example, the vertical column would have three phases of inquiry—exploration, integration, and resolution; while the performance levels could be judged by relevance (integral to thread), clarity (succinctness) and argument (references). For more ideas of discussion rubrics see Swan, Shen & Hiltz (2006).

Most course management systems provide tracking features that allow teachers to monitor the number of log-ons and contributions to online

Student: _____

Component	Beginning	Developing	Accomplished	Score
Participation	1 point Only contributed and participated in one of the online discussion forums	3 points Contributed and participated in three of the online discussion forums	5 points Contributed and participated in each of the five online discussion forums	
Moderation	1 point Posted an initial online discussion forum question	3 points Posted several discussion forum questions	5 points Posted several discussion forum questions and responded to the postings of other students	
Summary	3 points Provided a general summary of the online discussion forum	5 points Summarized the important ideas that emerged from the discussions	7 points Summarized the important ideas that emerged from the discussions, the unresolved and contentious topics, and key concepts that captured the discussion	
Resources	1 point Incomplete list of resources and citations	2 points Core list of resources cited in APA format	3 points Extensive and relevant list of resources cited in APA format	

Total score	/20

Figure 10.1 Discussion Rubric

forums. Thus, it is possible to compile data quickly about student participation. However, tabulating the number of postings is not an accurate measure of meaningful contributions or student achievement and growth. We are also aware of a tendency in formal education for some students to adopt "instrumental" attitudes towards learning, wherein they strategically focus only on teacher-defined outcomes. Like much quality educational research, quality student assessment is multifaceted and uses a variety of measuring devices. We next examine some of the means to assess participation and contribution.

The computer systems that underlie e-learning communications can fairly easily be used for quantitative analysis of student postings. Instructors who measure the number of postings, with few guidelines or feedback mechanisms for shaping the quality of the messages, usually succeed in getting participation, but it is unclear if this assessment influences the quality of the discourse and learning outcomes. A more pedagogically sound assessment of student participation would result from a qualitative assessment of student participation that displays student postings in context. When undertaking the task of assessing messages in context, one must be diligent to make the assessment criteria as visible as possible and to share these criteria at the beginning of the course.

The challenge for teachers is to be able to use criteria in a manner that is objective and that is replicable enough to meet students' and institutional needs. While it is argued here that such a task is achievable, from a practical perspective, caution must be exercised about recommending such activities because the implications for teacher workload are considerable. Since the ultimate goal of any formal education course is to induce learners to become cognizant of their own learning, it is possible to have students present their own evidence of meaningful participation in e-learning activities. Students should be given the opportunity to reflect on their contributions and progress in the community of inquiry. This can be shared in the form of an online journal or blog. Another tactic is metacognitively labeling their contributions according to the phases of the PI model which could then be a source for assessing the quality of contributions.

Students' own postings can be used as the basis for reflection on learning activities, and assessment (Davie, 1989; Paulsen, 1995). Typically, students are asked, at the end of the course, to illustrate both their contributions and evidence of learning by composing a "reflection piece" in which they quote from their own posting to the course. Students should be given guidance to help them extract quotations that illustrate their contributions. Obviously, students who have not participated will not be able to provide any transcript references from their own postings and, thus, will generally receive lower assessment ratings. Alternatively, a student may still be able to show learning by selective extraction of relevant postings, thus providing an opportunity to boost assessment ratings for the vicariously participating student (lurker).

Self-assessment of contributions can be further refined by having students undertake moderating functions during specific timeframes of the course. They can then be asked to demonstrate their contribution to the class and the discourse by quoting their contributions to teaching presence (such as summaries, welcoming comments, learning instigations, and other contributions). They should also be asked to reflect on their metacognitive knowledge and ability. Students could also be presented with a summary of social, cognitive, and teaching presence indicators and asked to describe to which of the three categories their postings contribute most significantly.

Assessment Activities

A quality community of inquiry e-learning experience contains a balanced set of learning activities that work individually and together to induce discourse and reflection. The e-learning environment can support a growing number of potential activities. Growing, because online technologies are continuing to evolve and support increased combinations of text, voice, and multimedia interaction that can occur in both synchronous and asynchronous formats. Palloff & Pratt (2009) provide examples of activities that include performance assessments (wikis), authentic assessments (real-world case studies), portfolio assessments (journal or blog), and online computer generated tests and quizzes. Furthermore, as a professional community, e-learning teachers are devising, testing, and sharing new learning activities.

 A common assignment in higher education is the assignment of finding, reading, and critiquing a relevant published article of particular interest to the student. This has several advantages of having students explore appropriate journals, select an article that is of interest, read the article for deep meaning, and then write a short review and critique. Guiding students and fairly assessing such work can be greatly facilitated through the use of an assessment rubric. Figure 10.2 shows a rubric designed to assess a reading assignment, developed by Norm Vaughan.

Consistent with the increased emphasis on active learning and authentic assessment is increased use of portfolios of learner products, or artifacts, in e-learning. Portfolios "evidence understanding of important concepts or mastery of key skills by requiring students to organize, synthesize, and communicate their achievements . . ." (Swan, Shen & Hiltz, 2006, p. 53). The construction of learning artifacts demonstrates knowledge acquisition in a very fundamental and explicit manner. It can include demonstration of individual understanding as well as collaborative contributions. Portfolio assessment also is congruent with strategies that allow significant input from students into their own learning goals. Students can then embark on individual and collaborative learning paths and demonstrate their accomplishment through the artifacts or evidence as demonstrated in their portfolio. The e-learning transcript can be used as one very useful component of the portfolio, and teachers can ask students to annotate, summarize, or otherwise add reflective metacognitive comments to their archived contributions.

Each of the activities and strategies employed to assess student learning has methodological and epistemological limitations. While using these strategies, we are attempting to measure complex domains of knowledge as they are instantiated in individual and collaborative contexts. It is important for assessment strategies to "ensure both group interdependence and individual accountability" (Swan, Shen & Hiltz, 2006, p. 53). Interdependent accountability may be as straightforward as documenting the sharing and use of resources. That said, a successful undertaking of these assessments is an immense challenge. Further, teachers are compelled to undertake these assessments in a transparent, reliable, and authentic manner that allows students or college administrators to challenge them. In order to reduce the error inherent in over-reliance on a single assessment activity, good instructors use

Student: _____

Component	Beginning	Developing	Accomplished	Score/ Comments
Synthesis/ Summary	1 point Incomplete synthesis — missing components	2 points All components of the synthesis are present but not completely developed, including the: • principal question, argument or thesis statement • theoretical framework • methodology • study findings • conclusion and/or recommendations	3 points A complete and fully developed synthesis of the article	
Critique	1 point Incomplete critique — missing components	3 points All components of the critique are present but not completely developed including a discussion of: • the validity and reliability of the study findings • why you agree or disagree with conclusion/ recommendations	6 points A complete and fully developed critique of the article	

Figure 10.2 Article Critique Rubric

	1 point	3 points	7 points	
Reflection	Incomplete reflection — missing components	All components of the reflection are present but not completely developed, including: • comments about what you took away from this article • ideas on how you could apply the findings, conclusion, and recommendations from this article to develop your own blended learning course/program	A complete and fully developed reflection of the article	
	1 point	**2 points**	**4 points**	
Organization	Ideas are not presented in a clear fashion and the article critique lacks organization	Ideas are presented clearly but the student takes too long coming to the point and the article lacks organization	The article critique is organized in a logical fashion with ideas clearly and concisely stated	
	2 points	**6 points**	**10 points**	
Peer review of an article critique	Incomplete review — missing components	All components of the peer review are present but not completely developed, including comments on: • what you learned from reviewing the article critique • what you enjoyed about this critique (and why) • what recommendations or advice would you like to share with the person who created this critique (e.g., future ideas, ways to improve the next article critique)	A complete and fully developed peer review of the article critique	
Total score				**/30**

Figure 10.2 continued

a variety of assessments throughout the course. This variety should occur in the format of assessment: quizzes, short answer, longer articulated response, and term paper; in the degree of collaboration required from individual to group assignments; in the role of assessor from self to peer to teacher assessment; and from assessing broad theoretical understanding to assessing very practical applications of new knowledge.

There is a growing interest in using problem-based inquiry learning activities in e-learning education. Problem-based inquiry learning focuses learning by confronting students with ill-structured problems that mirror, as closely as possible, real issues and concerns from an authentic domain. The teacher's role in problem-based inquiry learning is, first, to construct authentic problems. These problems are based on curriculum or the domain of knowledge about which students are expected to gain knowledge and competency. The instructor then seeks out, and makes available, an appropriate set of resources that students can use to find solutions to the problem. As noted previously, case studies are excellent examples of a problem-based activity. They encourage students to be actively involved in their learning as problem solvers, as opposed to content receivers found in dissemination-based educational approaches.

During the problem-based inquiry learning process, the teacher acts as a coach and a role model. Coaching functions include helping students to attack the problem at the correct level, assisting with structuring and documenting their tentative solutions, and helping students organize their learning activities in other ways. Of course, problem-based inquiry learning inevitably includes false starts and trips down paths that are unproductive; however, the instructor should not short circuit this important component of the inquiry process. The instructor thus acts as a co-investigator in the problem solution, fading into the background as students' ability to solve problems without intervention grows.

Student assessment in problem-based inquiry learning contexts is more challenging than assessing traditional educational outcomes in terms of content acquisition. Problem-based inquiry learning attempts to induce deep levels of learning and to develop students' self-directed and metacognitive learning abilities. As such, simple measures of knowledge retention are not able to assess student growth in these important areas. Because of this, a variety of assessment activities are often built into problem-based inquiry learning. These can include presentations in which students demonstrate or post their solutions to the problem, self and peer assessments in which students assess their own contributions and the contributions of other group members, and the development of concept maps that document problem solutions and the processes used to achieve those solutions.

Problem-based inquiry learning in an e-learning context is not significantly different to that which is orchestrated in a classroom setting. However, since most problem-based inquiry learning activities are structured to allow group investigation, the needs for supporting group synchronization, document management, discussion, and task assignment must be supported. Providing opportunities for synchronous activity through real-time audio or text chat is helpful for students to plan and undertake group activities efficiently. In environments that are based solely on asynchronous interaction it is often difficult for groups to allocate tasks quickly and plan their problem-solving activities. Time must be allotted accordingly and facilitation provided on the front end.

Finally, one of the inherent advantages of community-based learning models is the capacity to discuss the critical role of assessment with students. In most cases of higher learning, e-learning should not be reduced to machine-marked assessment of teacher-defined assessment criteria. Rather, the inherent communications capacity of the Internet can be used to allow students to comment upon, focus, and negotiate the type of assessment so that students understand the purpose, and understand that it adequately reflects and guides their learning objectives. Student input and control of the learning program is central to effective higher education. If students are expected to assume increasing control of their learning, they must have some choice over the content and process. This control must extend beyond choice of goals to choice of how these goals are assessed.

COURSE EVALUATION

Assessment of student learning is a key component of the evaluation of an online course, but it is only one of the factors with which educators involved in e-learning are concerned. The e-learning context is complex and made up of many components. All these components must work together in a seamless fashion if quality educational outcomes are to be realized. Palloff & Pratt (2009) list eight elements when evaluating an online course:

- perception of the course experience;
- orientation to the course;
- quality and quantity of content;
- discussion and interaction;
- self-assessment of participation and performance;
- course management system;
- technical support;
- access to resources.

Obviously, adequately evaluating a course of studies is a challenging endeavor.

Evaluation begins by determining the strategic intent of the e-learning program. In this regard, clearly identifying why the particular e-learning course has been developed and delivered is crucial to assessing its effectiveness. Traditionally, distance education courses have been offered in order to increase public access to formal education opportunities by spanning geographic or temporal distance. While access is a component of e-learning, the potential of e-learning speaks to issues of quality as a function of interactive and collaborative capabilities. Institutions also attempt to use e-learning as a means to increase revenues, to increase or retain market share of students, and to enhance institutional or national recognition or prestige. Obviously, the knowledge of the potential of e-learning is critical to establishing mechanisms for measuring the achievement of these goals. It should be noted that these goals are often hidden and implicit (Anderson, 2001); therefore, the first role of the educator must be to explicate these hidden agendas.

Another element in proactive evaluation is to look closely at the content of the courses. Sims (2001) points out that content for any course exists along a continuum from the static content that is predetermined by the course developer–instructor, before any students are enrolled, to content that is totally constructed by the contributions of the students and teacher as the course progresses. Each component of this content must be congruent with other components so that a cohesive and easily understood package results. For example, writing style should be consistent and match the reading level and the degree of familiarity with vocabulary appropriate to the average learner enrolled in the course. The content of the course material must be accurate and all authors should acknowledge any bias they bring to the discussion. While this seems to be a common-sense requirement it can become problematic as the learners contribute content in collaborative environments.

Effective evaluation of e-learning material requires a close examination of the instructional design incorporated in the course. E-learning courses reflect the pedagogical biases and understandings of their creators. There are many examples of e-learning content that is based on instructivist designs but masquerading as constructivist designs. Despite differences in design, every course should be aligned with the prior experience and knowledge of the learners; should provide pathways and sequencing that are coherent, clear, and complete; should provide opportunities for discourse; should provide means by which both students and teachers can assess their learning and the expected outcomes; and the ways in which these outcomes are to be achieved should be clearly articulated.

Specific to the point of this chapter, course evaluation should address evaluating the quality, quantity, and thoroughness of the assessment of student learning. As discussed previously, assessment drives much learning behavior and in many ways defines the course—at least as perceived by student participants. A proactive evaluation of the course looks closely at the assessment activities and notes how accurately they measure both the espoused and the hidden course objectives. Most quality courses will have multiple forms of assessment, including assessment of both individual and group work. The means by which the evaluation is authenticated against discipline or community norms is also a concern.

The degree of student support forms the next element of course evaluation. Since students are unique, there is an infinite number of issues that may impede student learning during e-learning courses. To overcome these impediments, a variety of student support services must be available in conjunction with quality e-learning courses. These resources need to focus on the content (remedial activities for some and enrichment for other students), on technical issues (especially if the technology used for delivery support is novel, sophisticated, or complex), and on personal issues (various types of counseling support).

The final area of course evaluation relates to assessing the degree to which outcomes have been met. Are the learners satisfied with the courses? Are credentialing or accreditation organizations able to certify those who have successfully completed the courses? Are teachers satisfied with the work conditions and the workloads associated with the course? Are there mechanisms in place so that the course will be continuously improved during subsequent iterations? It may also be relevant to evaluate whether the course is affordable to students, cost effective for the institution, and makes a difference to the students.

CONCLUSION

As the breadth of the discussion above illustrates, judging the worth of an e-learning experience is a broad and complex topic that includes much more than merely assessing student performance outcomes and their perceptions of the value of the course. Rigorous evaluation is justified given the complexity and novelty of the development and delivery of e-learning in a community of inquiry environment. It is only through rigorous and systematic evaluation efforts that we will be able to develop our understanding of the many complex e-learning issues.

Chapter 11

Organizational Issues

Many institutions of higher education have purposely begun to position themselves with regards to e-learning. They have made serious efforts to move ahead from the public relations rhetoric associated with innovation toward becoming leaders in drafting vision, policies, and goals with regard to e-learning. These institutions have begun to question and redefine their conceptions of what constitutes a quality learning experience in the context of ubiquitous, mediated communications environments and have begun to understand where such innovations really do add value. The answer to the question of what distinguishes institutions of higher education is increasingly being seen in terms of the context and process of learning (i.e., communities of learners); not simply access to content. By revisiting their core values and culture, these institutions are recognizing a need to move away from passive lectures and are realizing that e-learning may be the catalyst and means to enhance the scholarly culture and learning environment significantly.

Expectations are changing and there is little doubt that institutions of higher education are being transformed as a result of e-learning innovations. However, the question is how transformation will be led and managed. Institutions face the challenge of developing a vision and strategic direction that will position them to move forward while not reducing their agility to adapt to new innovations. Meeting this challenge demands insightful and resourceful organizational leadership.

STRATEGIC INNOVATION

E-learning is not an experiment. It has moved into the mainstream of higher education and is recognized as a strategic asset. The reason for this is the recognition of the pressing need to address inherent deficiencies in higher education related to over-reliance on lectures and information dissemination. The important implication is that the real value-add is not simply course content, but the communicative quality of the learning experience. In short, the purpose of innovation must be the enhancement of the quality of the learning environment. Competition in higher education will be about quality, and e-learning will be at the heart of this challenge. More time and effort, however, must be expended on understanding e-learning and how it can serve core values and enhance quality. Too much effort continues to be expended to sustain the *status quo* and too little time is given to developing strategies to enhance the quality of the learning experience.

Katz (2010) states that the digital age will reshape higher education and the "leaders of today's traditional scholarly enterprises must rethink a number of fundamentals behind the higher education institution" (p. 52). One area that Katz argues must be rethought is the value proposition of "place." Traditionally, higher education institutions were defined by place in terms of where the repositories of knowledge physically existed. Clearly in the digital age this proposition no longer holds. The challenge is to "convey how place factors into the student experience" (Katz, 2010, p. 53). Place, however, is more than physical presence. It is a sense of being connected to and belonging to a scholarly community. From the perspective of the traditional educational experience, place will initially be addressed by embracing blended learning (face to face and online) and then extending the academic community through the possibilities of e-learning.

It is not an option to suggest that an institution is campus based and, therefore, e-learning is not relevant. E-learning pervades, and will transform, all teaching and learning whether it is face to face, blended, or online. Most importantly, it has the real potential to enhance the traditional values and ethos of higher education by fostering communities of learners and the integration of research into the curriculum. Traditional higher education teaching and learning practices that limit engagement (i.e., the lecture) put institutions at a serious disadvantage pedagogically. E-learning is eroding the credibility of passive information transmission approaches inherent in most higher education institutions. The challenge for institutions is to adopt what is, in the short term, a disruptive technology.

E-learning is a disruptive technology in traditional institutions of higher education because it threatens the sustaining technology—the lecture. Disruptive technologies are invariably a threat to established organizations, and in the longer term if they do not adjust will be the source of their demise (Christensen, 1997). According to Christensen, disruptive technologies have caused dominant firms to fail because those firms have refused, for whatever reasons, to adapt to them. The challenge for these organizations is to transform themselves during periods of technological change. Such fundamental change is currently being experienced in higher education. It is becoming ever more evident that e-learning's ability to facilitate an enhanced, yet more convenient and in many cases less expensive educational approach, is not mere hyperbole. The survival of many higher education institutions will depend on how they address this transformational challenge.

The winning strategy is to find relatively low-risk niche areas in which the technology can be understood and incubated and where, if there are failures, they will come early and be less expensive. From a business perspective, Christensen (1997) suggests, the "innovator's task is to ensure that this innovation . . . is taken seriously . . . without putting at risk the needs of present customers . . ." (p. xxiv).

> Attention to new, disruptive technologies should not preclude sufficient attention being paid to the sustaining technologies that will allow the central core of the institution to maintain its favorable position in the marketplace.
>
> (Archer, Garrison & Anderson, 1999, p. 24)

This perspective makes perfect sense in an educational institution. When innovating e-learning, the legitimate needs of campus-based learners and the core values of the faculty and the institution must be recognized or the disruptive technology will be greatly resisted—even at the institution's own peril. Academic leadership has a very challenging balancing task that must begin with development of sound policy and ownership of the innovation.

Policy Development

Many universities are making substantial, albeit fragmented, investments in e-learning. However, because of the lack of a strategic direction, coherent approach, and sustained commitment, there is little to show in terms of fundamental change. Concurrent with incubating e-learning as a disruptive technology, institutional policy must be developed to provide direction and to focus sufficient resources to facilitate what will be a long and difficult process—the transformation of the sustaining technologies and vested interests of a large institution.

Some of the topics that a policy document and strategic plan should include are:

1 Vision:

   - understand background;
   - define core values;
   - describe strategic goals.

2 Needs and risk assessment:

   - identify issues;
   - identify challenges;
   - identify best practices.

3 Educational principles and outcomes described.
4 Implementation initiatives and strategy:

- link to institutional priorities;
- create a steering committee;
- identify communities of practice.

5 Infrastructure:

- design multi-media classrooms;
- describe administrative processes.

6 Support services:

- provide professional development;
- provide learner support.

7 Resources, incentives and recognition.
8 Benchmarking and research:

- establish success criteria;
- assess progress;
- communicate direction and accomplishments.

While space does not allow for a thorough discussion of each of these points, there are several issues that must be addressed to ensure that an e-learning vision and strategic plan are effectively created and implemented. First, the vision and strategic plan must have a few attainable goals and initiatives that have the support of the institution's leaders. Strategies must be seen as flexible actions that will inevitably need to be rethought and reshaped as the realities of implementation are presented. Second, there must be collaborative leadership throughout the entire process that includes senior leaders. Taking a more inclusive approach will provide an opportunity to build trust and create a sense of ownership. Third, research and evaluation is necessary to remain current and to stay on track. This is really a corollary of the first point in that implementation of a strategy must be continually informed with new ideas internally and externally. Finally, considerable effort must be given to communication to sustain the collaborative leadership (ensure that e-learning remains a priority), that successes are shared, and that support is maintained.

Lasting innovation does not occur from the top down nor does it grow from the bottom up. More often than not, effecting change is an iterative process where middle-level leaders (who have the expertise and commitment) with the sustained collaboration of both senior management and the grass roots are in a position to provide realistic strategic input. The vision must have strategic and practical value and be seen to be an imperative. Moreover, for leadership to commit to this vision, they must see the potential benefits and be assured of success. This means that senior leadership must be provided with evaluation data on a sustained basis in which they can be assured of success. Only with this commitment will policy and resources be directed to the systemic integration of e-learning.

INFRASTRUCTURE

It should be clear that a vision and strategic plan must be systemic. It is not sufficient to select elements of the strategic plan in a fragmented or *ad hoc* manner. All the elements of the plan must be integrated in a coherent and timely manner. The system and conceptual approach that will best integrate the essential elements of an e-learning culture is a learning experience with communities of practice at its core. Learning management systems can create an enabling environment and provide much of the functionality for e-learning. This should not be a surprise when we realize that higher education is about creating knowledge as well as managing its preservation and dissemination. Learning management is the needed "middle ware" that links repositories and the educational process. It is the infrastructure that will empower the communities of practice that will ultimately provide the buy-in and sustainability of e-learning.

Equally important is the recognition and integration of communities of practice where teachers and students can manage and share information and knowledge with regard to curriculum, course management, and pedagogical processes. Knowledge management builds upon the foundation of a collaborative community of inquiry that involves both creation and application of knowledge (know-how embedded in the wisdom of practice). As Rosenberg (2001) states, the "importance of community cannot be overstated" and its real power "is that it creates opportunities for people to go beyond interaction with content to contributing information and sharing . . ." (p. 80). That is, knowledge management encourages members of the community to consider new ideas, grow, and innovate.

As alluded to previously, institutional investment in e-learning and associated infrastructure will require not only the full commitment of senior administration but the leadership of a person with status and vision. Successful innovation demands strong leadership.

LEADERSHIP

It has been commonly understood that higher education stands apart in its determination to resist change and the effective use of technology (Duderstadt,

Atkins & Van Houweling, 2002). However, the call for change in higher education is different today (Piper, 2008). While there are traditions in higher education that should be protected, there are legitimate calls for change when it comes to outdated approaches to teaching and the need to engage students in the educational process. It is argued that what is missing in higher education when it comes to much needed innovation in teaching and learning is leadership.

E-learning is at the center of a transformation in teaching and learning in higher education. In times of fundamental change, successful transformation depends upon effective leadership. There is a core set of leadership values and characteristics required to integrate e-learning fully into the institutional mainstream in higher education. The values and personal virtues essential to a leader are integrity and openness. Successful leaders treat people with fairness, honesty, openness, and respect. These values and virtues may be manifested in numerous ways. The characteristics we focus on here are vision, commitment, decisiveness, and the ability to recognize talent. These leadership qualities instill the confidence in others to provide the knowledge and action to effect worthwhile change.

First, leadership must have a vision and be willing to advocate for change. This vision must then be translated into understandable and achievable strategic goals and actions. Next, leadership must show commitment to action and a willingness to make difficult decisions. Commitment to action reflects decisiveness. Decisiveness is a corollary to change that requires conviction and mediates vision and action. Decisiveness represents the courage to move forward with the expectation that adjustments will need to be made. The future can never be predicted and, consequently, surprises and failures will inevitably occur along the way. Leadership will expect these setbacks, accept them and learn from them, and move on.

While innovation is commonplace, true transformation occurs only rarely. Adopting e-learning in its full potential is a transformative process that requires a sustained commitment to overcome inevitable resistance. Decisiveness is having the courage to make timely decisions, to seize opportunities, invariably without as much information or consultation as is desirable, or even prudent. Leadership must listen and reflect very carefully but not be afraid to take the all-essential first step. Innovation and transformation do not emerge from consensus but, rather, consensus results from open communication and collaboration.

Open communication and an ability to listen can identify and refine ideas. However, the value of collaboration is to enhance individual creativity, responsibility, and action. One of the great secrets of successful leadership is being able to recognize talent and work collaboratively with that talent. There is no substitute for talent. All it may take is a few key, dedicated and talented individuals in the right places and willing to work together to initiate worthwhile innovation that can be contagious.

Collaborative Leadership

Change requires strong leadership. Not only is higher education in need of a commitment to change, but there is a need for a new kind of leadership. Change goes to the heart of leadership—otherwise all we need are good administrators. Fundamental change associated with e-learning is dependent upon new ideas and new leadership approaches. Successful implementation of e-learning to address outdated teaching is predicated upon a new approach—collaborative leadership. Collaborative leadership pulls together leaders at all levels of the institution. It means encouraging input and creating ownership through a collaboratively developed vision and plan. Collaborative leadership also means shared responsibility for the results. Through such an approach to leadership real commitment can be sustained.

We know the professed personal qualities of a leader—vision, integrity, openness, and courage—but these individual qualities are no longer sufficient. Leadership is not just about the exceptional characteristics of a leader. These characteristics can only manifest themselves in a culture of shared purpose and collaboration. The charismatic leader who single-handedly transforms an organization is largely fictional. Perhaps the most important characteristic of today's leader is an authentic desire and ability to work collaboratively and constructively toward strategic goals. Effective leadership in higher education must develop shared commitment and productive relationships. Collaborative leadership brings together a group purposely to explore ideas and test solutions in a climate of trust. Collaborative leadership emulates that of a community of inquiry.

Much can be learned from the concepts associated with the CoI theoretical framework with regard to the dynamics of collaborative leadership. Collaborative leadership occurs in a community with the goal to create a sense of purpose and commitment in focusing on strategic change and finding solutions to pressing problems. This search for solutions is core to the process of inquiry. Inquiry provides the means for individuals to contribute to addressing a problem and subsequently finding ownership in a vision and strategic direction. The objective here is to explore leadership through the lens of a community of inquiry and, specifically, the three elements of a community of inquiry.

It is the task of true leadership to create a sense of purpose and cohesion through open communication and trust. These are the characteristics of social presence that have been shown to be essential to a community of inquiry. It is also the means to create a safe environment to address challenges honestly and share ideas for change. Only collaborative leadership that allows others to share commitment and responsibility will realize the concerted effort required to transform teaching and learning in higher education. As Weigel (2002) states, "Robust communities of inquiry that make education an exciting experience for both students and educators can hardly take root in organizational cultures marked by isolation, fear, territoriality, and power plays" (p. 127). Unfortunately, this is too often the case in many higher education institutions. Isolation and fear can only be overcome through open communication, cohesion, and trusting relationships.

Collaboration to resolve a dilemma or problem is the focus of the inquiry process and the purpose of leadership. Practical inquiry (cognitive presence) is a collaborative process where new ideas can emerge and be tested. This is the workplace for collaborative leadership. Collaborative leadership is not about imposing a vision and dictating action plans. It is a process where participants first come to understand the issues, clarify the facts, and critically analyze solutions to build consensus. However, agreement with regard to a vision is only the beginning. The inquiry process begins anew as participants address the task of creating a strategic action plan that is scalable and sustainable. This is where commitment and buy-in is essential. When it comes to change in teaching and learning, communication with the institutional community must be ongoing. In terms of a strategic action plan, there is a need to set strategic objectives, offer incentives, focus scarce resources, and provide professional development.

It is recognized that a community of inquiry must have strong leadership as evidenced through the teaching presence construct. Teaching presence is in essence collaborative leadership. It has been labeled teaching and not teacher presence because others also have the potential and responsibility to assume the leadership role in a community of inquiry. All members of the community need to participate in the leadership function. At the same time, it is explicitly recognized that there must be strong direction. This reflects the role of a strong leader—a leader who works collaboratively but recognizes his or her responsibility to take control when required to move the process forward and ensure the goals are realized in an expeditious manner. The characteristics of teaching presence in a community of inquiry are those same features that shape the collaborative leadership that is so greatly needed in higher education if we are to address the need for transformative change in how we meaningfully engage students in the learning process.

Before concluding this section on leadership, it may be useful to remind ourselves of the challenge of significant change in institutions that have traditionally resisted change. It has famously been stated "that there is nothing more difficult to carry out, nor more doubtful of success, nor more dangerous to handle, than to initiate a new order of things" (Machiavelli, in Green, 1998, p. 396). This would surely be a fair comment about transforming teaching and learning in higher education. The point is that we need recognize the challenges associated with the adoption of e-learning and the courage required of our leaders to affect a "new order of things."

In keeping with the challenge, it is only realistic to expect that transformation associated with the adoption of e-learning will inevitably take an incremental approach. It is unrealistic to think that e-learning will somehow, overnight, magically transform teaching and learning in higher education. As important as collaborative leadership is to change in higher education, it must also be sustainable. One of the realities in higher education is that leadership changes on a frequent basis. While it can be advantageous for new leaders to bring new ideas and energy to the process, too often it means shifting to new priorities with the loss of considerable investment of time, resources, and momentum, not to mention the risk of demoralizing faculty. Leaders must give innovation time before we can expect it to spread and become a contagion (Gladwell, 2002).

Another observation about change is that e-learning innovation is a direct challenge to the lecture. Questioning the lecture is hard to accept for most professors when this is basically the only model that they know or have experienced. Moving away from the lecture is doubly challenging as it is also a move away from transmitting excessive amounts of content. Add to this the challenge of coping with various new and emerging communication and information technologies, essential for an inquiry-based and engaged approach to learning, and this move may be an unacceptable confrontation for faculty. It is totally unrealistic to ask a professor to find the time to learn how to use this technology without professional development and support. This is just a non-starter for most professors.

Therefore, faculty must be supported through the entire process of designing and delivering an e-learning course. Instructional designers and technology support experts have to be there for them every step of the way. Here again is where the CoI theoretical framework can be enormously useful to structure workshops and guide faculty through the course redesign process (Vaughan & Garrison, 2006). The idea is to create a community where faculty can be introduced to the key elements of a community of inquiry and experience the kind of trusting environment that they need to create for their students. Through this process a network of sustained support can be created. Support, however, must also be accompanied by incentives and scholarly recognition of faculty who take the risk and invest enormous amounts of time and energy in fundamentally redesigning their courses.

Finally, a major factor in the ability to innovate and adopt new approaches to teaching and learning has to be visionary leadership and commitment to what has become the obvious need for fundamental change. There is no excuse for indecision. The need and direction for change is apparent to those leaders who choose to see and comprehend. Leadership must get beyond the rhetoric and address true innovation. The rhetoric is that the student is the most important stakeholder in higher education, but the reality often says something very different. The reality is that classes, or should we say lectures, have simply become larger with minimal accommodation to address engagement and communication opportunities with the professor. This is now the time for collaborative leadership and a commitment to action.

CONCLUSION

In the coming together of the information era and knowledge society, institutions must be prepared to focus greater attention on the strategic integration of e-learning. Institutions of higher education need to rediscover their roots and ideals. This may well require constructing and communicating the vision and strategic plan in the face of considerable resistance. To be successful, leaders must understand the dynamics of change and be prepared to start small but successfully. They must recognize and incubate e-learning as a disruptive technology, while demonstrating how it can meet the challenges and demands of the future.

Chapter 12

Future Directions

We need to stop being seduced by technology and trivial applications masquerading as an educational experience. Much of what we have experienced during the first decade of the 21st century is an infatuation with personal information and communication made possible by ubiquitous and inexpensive technologies. We have seen unimagined developments in how we can communicate and express our opinions any time and anywhere through social networking. The challenge going forward is to understand how these technological developments can be used in the service of the ideals and values of higher education.

The reduced cost of storage and bandwidth were the big technological advances in the first decade of this century. This provided an enormous database and virtually instantaneous access to information. However, broadly speaking, these advances were largely in the service of entertainment and social communication. While there were some who were using the technology to reflect, share ideas, and engage in discourse, most were not engaged in the creation of knowledge—they were largely consumers of random facts and titillating bits of information made possible by social networks. It was a decade of turmoil as communication technologies were transforming society. It was also a decade of confusion for educational institutions in terms of what to make of these technological developments.

From an educational perspective, one positive outcome is that society has come to accept the ubiquitous presence of mediated communication. Technology adoption no longer brings with it the same resistance it once did. While most of us remain intimidated and often frustrated by new technologies, we have come to accept their inevitable role in society. This is certainly true in business and the home, but technology's influence in the educational sector remains on the periphery and its potential is largely unrealized. The problem is that in the past educators focused too much on the technology and not enough on examining the deficiencies, limitations, and dissatisfaction with the existing pedagogical practices common in higher education. The question is not what technology can do but what are the educational needs. That is, we did not fully analyze our educational needs before asking how technology could address deficiencies and support legitimate educational goals.

In the final analysis, e-learning is not about technology; it is about what we truly value as a higher educational experience. As powerfully enabling as the new and emerging technologies are, and will be, their adoption should always be about approaching the ideals of a higher educational experience. Ideals that will also develop the ability of individuals to adapt to a society based on creating and constructing knowledge. In this regard, large undergraduate lectures face an existential crisis and, as a result, higher education is facing a significant transformational challenge. An e-learning community of inquiry is a transformative framework that will significantly shift the approach to learning in higher education.

The adoption of e-learning has entered a period of positive educational and technological realism. That is, realism in terms of an appreciation of the enormous potential of e-learning but also recognition of the educational and pedagogical challenges to change the embedded passive information transmission approach that still dominates undergraduate higher education.

THE FIRST DECADE

The first decade of e-learning was spent experiencing the new. The focus was on learning to manipulate the technology and seeing what it could do. As inevitably happens, however, the technology got ahead of the pedagogy. Many in education were forced to reflect upon the implications of the Internet and communications technology for the field of education. For a few, there was a period of innovation and experimentation to understand how the potential of communications technology could be used to enhance educational environments. At the same time, e-learning was perhaps over-hyped as new online learning institutions proliferated. However, most of these did not survive and e-learning had a limited influence on campus-based higher education institutions. This was certainly true in the early years of the decade as we attempted to grasp its properties and educational potential.

A turning point, however, for the adoption of e-learning in higher education was the idea of blended or hybrid educational designs. That is, the thoughtful integration of online and face-to-face approaches. The evidence of the potential of blended learning opened the eyes of many in higher education and provided the confidence to take e-learning to the next level (Means, Toyama, Murphy, Bakia & Jones, 2009; Twigg, 2003). It did not mitigate, however, the challenges of integrating e-learning approaches in higher education institutions.

E-learning came of age during the first decade of this century. It evolved from several decades of experimentation with computer conferencing and the advent of the Internet. The publication of the Community of Inquiry framework (Garrison, Anderson & Archer, 2000) marked the transition from a specific application of e-learning (computer conferencing) to a comprehensive consideration of asynchronous collaboration for educational purposes. It also marked a shift from an obsession with social presence to a perspective that considered the dynamic interplay of social, cognitive, and teaching presence in a collaborative constructivist educational environment. After a decade of research using the Community of Inquiry theoretical framework, we have a reasonably good understanding of the process of creating and sustaining online and blended communities of learners.

The end of this decade was marked by the term Web 2.0 and the focus on the Web as a platform for collaboration. Notwithstanding the technological focus of Web 2.0, these tools opened the door for various social networking applications and the opportunity to create sustainable communities of inquiry. It is the realization of the educational ideals associated with communities of learners that we will experience as we move into the next decade. It will be an exciting and transformative age for higher education. The idea of creating and sustaining communities of inquiry represents the conceptual transition to the second decade of e-learning in this century.

THE SECOND DECADE

The predictions for fundamental change in higher education and even the demise of the university campus (Tapscott, 1996), so prominent at the turn of the century, simply did not happen. This is why it is impossible to predict the impact of technological innovation. Katz (2010, p. 44) eloquently reflects this limitation to predict the future with regard to technological change:

> . . . the lens on the future has always been a cloudy one. We see through the glass darkly. Discovering later that we have understated the enormity of change wrought by existing or unimagined technologies while we have overstated the pace of change.

At best we can extrapolate from the present in order to provide some practical value of how to prepare for the near future. As argued above, the digital revolution did not reach into mainstream higher education due largely to the infatuation with the technology *per se*. However, this is not the end of the story. A prediction with greater credibility is that the "industrial model of pedagogy" (largely in the form of a lecture) is becoming obsolete and the transformation of the university is an imperative—"further delay may be dire" (Tapscott & Williams, 2010, p. 16).

> Universities are losing their grip on higher learning as the Internet is, inexorably, becoming the dominant infrastructure for knowledge—both

> as a container and as a global platform for knowledge exchange between people—and as a new generation of students requires a very different model of higher education.
>
> (Tapscott & Williams, 2010, p. 16)

The authors argue that a perfect storm is brewing and attention must be focused on how faculty and students interact. Higher education "cannot survive on lectures alone" (Tapscott & Williams, 2010, p. 20).

The second decade of the 21st century will mark a move away from the myth and hype of the predictions at the turn of the century. It will be a decade where we begin to realize the potential of the Internet and communications technology for a new educational model. It will be a time when the culture of the educational community begins to shift and particular institutions will sort through the hype and turn the vision and need for collaborative inquiry into reality. Higher education courses and programs will start by integrating blended learning approaches. E-learning will be absorbed into the mainstream and become core to achieving the traditional ideals of higher learning in terms of realizing sustainable learning communities. E-learning will become an integral aspect of academic life—in terms of both the classroom and campus life. Engagement will take on a new and richer meaning academically and socially.

As we enter the age of technological adolescence in higher education, educators are becoming more aware and responsible in terms of applying technology with greater understanding and purpose. While technological advances will continue, providing educators with more (and less expensive) communication choices will see substantive applications of technology. This will certainly be the case in the field of higher education as we come to accept the need for change in how we design and deliver educational experiences that correspond to the needs of a changing society. Pressure has come to bear on the educational community to address quality concerns and relevancy issues. However, many in the educational community will continue to resist the need to transform the educational experience. Educational leaders will not come to this willingly. This has enormous resource challenges and implications for managing change. At the same time, the larger educational community (including students) will become increasingly restive as they turn away from passive information transmission models.

With regard to the promises of e-learning, Pittinsky (2003) made the prediction that "universities will maintain ubiquitous Web environments that are personalized, are cohesive, are as critical to the campus community as the quad of old, and can be the spark for a renewed focus on social networks in the educational process" (p. 215). First, it can be cautiously stated that this prediction has been largely realized. Clearly most universities have a ubiquitous Web environment where students can create personalized portals. The decade of research on the Community of Inquiry theoretical framework reported here indicates that coherent communities can and are being created for academic and social purposes.

Extrapolating into the future we can see social media increasingly becoming the "university quad" where students can meet and create a sense of belonging and loyalty to the institution. This sense of community has been shown to be crucial for student satisfaction and persistence. Looking into the future this may well be the important contribution of social media. In general, Web 2.0 technologies will evolve into more sophisticated and powerful tools and have an enormous influence in higher education. With regard to social media in particular, they will become an essential element in creating an institutional environment that welcomes students, strengthens educational values, and grows relationships that support the academic goals of the students and the learning community. A connected campus life serves the aims of all.

FUTURE RESEARCH

The Community of Inquiry theoretical framework has been a successful catalyst and guide to a wide range of research into e-learning during the last decade (see Swan & Ice, 2010). The CoI theoretical framework continues to be invaluable in formulating relevant hypotheses and interpreting research findings. Based on the findings of the research reported here we identify areas ripe for future research in e-learning generally and the theory of the Community of Inquiry specifically.

Social Presence

While social presence has been the focus of research from the emergence of computer conferencing, there is still work to be done to understand its importance in the dynamics of a community of inquiry and its relationship to teaching and cognitive presence. Social presence has been shown to be an important mediating variable between teaching presence and cognitive presence (Garrison, Cleveland-Innes & Fung, 2010; Shea & Bidjerano, 2009a). This suggests that social presence is an important motivational variable that has considerable influence in group cohesion and persistence. In this regard, there is evidence that, in fact, social presence is a good predictor of persistence (Diaz, Swan, Ice & Kupczynski, 2010).

While there is evidence that the multidimensionality of social presence is relatively stable (Garrison, 2009b; Kim, in press), there is a need to confirm and refine the dimensions. More specifically, there is a considerable challenge to understand the dynamic and progressive nature of the dimensions of social presence. What are the differential effects or order of importance of each of the dimensions as a community of inquiry develops? For example, what should have precedence when creating a community of inquiry and establishing group cohesion—academic identity (course goals) or shared social identity (interpersonal relationships)? There is some evidence that group or course identity may be more important at the beginning of a course, while social identity or personal relationships may help sustain a community of inquiry over time (see Chapter 5).

Cognitive Presence

An area of research associated with cognitive presence is that of exploring the relationships between learning processes as measured by the phases of cognitive presence and actual learning outcomes. While there are challenges in measuring specific higher-order learning outcomes, the CoI theoretical framework has not failed as a model for learning outcomes (Akyol, Garrison & Ozden, 2009). Without reiterating the initial evidence here that has demonstrated a link between the PI model and learning outcomes (Akyol & Garrison, in press a), this is an area that is in need of vigorous research. As described below, the development of a quantitative instrument has opened up any number of possibilities to study learning outcomes as they relate to each of the presences and a community of inquiry as a whole.

Another interesting area of cognitive presence research is that of metacognition and the role it plays in practical inquiry. There is clearly a strong metacognitive element in the process of successful inquiry. As discussed in Chapter 6, for inquiry to reach the resolution phase, students must have a good sense of metacognitive awareness. The inquiry process can be greatly facilitated with metacognitive awareness of the inquiry cycle and expectations. To aid in the exploration of metacognitition, there is a need to continue with the development of a metacognitive construct. With such a construct it becomes possible to rigorously explore the relationships metacognition has with the PI cycle (cognitive presence) and also with teaching presence in terms of the development of metacognitive awareness.

Teaching Presence

One consistent finding over the last decade of research into the CoI theoretical framework is the importance of and central role that teaching presence plays in the development of a community of inquiry (Akyol & Garrison, 2008; Diaz et al., 2010; Garrison et al., 2010; Shea & Bidjerano, 2009a). It is central to establishing and maintaining both social and cognitive presence and higher-order learning. This research points out the need for a new line of research to establish the causal relationships among the presences; with particular focus on the role of teaching presence and its sub-elements of design, facilitation, and direction. This is central to a better understanding of the dynamics of a community of inquiry.

Another area of teaching presence research is associated with the dimensionality of the teaching presence construct. While studies have validated a three-dimensional teaching presence construct (Garrison & Arbaugh, 2007), other studies suggest teaching presence may be perceived by students as having two dimensions. Complicating this is that two different studies suggest conflation among the dimensions but with two different combinations among the three dimensions; that is, in one study students were not able to distinguish between facilitation and direct instruction (Shea, Li & Pickett, 2006); and, in another study, there was a question as to whether students conflated design and direct instruction (Ice, Arbaugh, Diaz, Garrison, Richardson, Shea & Swan, 2007). Uncertainty with regard to the structure of teaching presence is reinforced in another study that states that factor loadings "seem to bifurcate the teaching presence items" (Diaz et al., 2010, p. 27).

Practically speaking, another area of study with regard to teaching presence is the balance between facilitation and direct instruction during the progression of a course of study. There is evidence to suggest that too much direct instruction too early will discourage participation. Moderating and shaping the direction of the discourse are important educational responsibilities that must be properly balanced as learning progresses. Similarly, how important is it that, and when should, an instructor model critical discourse and metacognitive thinking?

While it is suggested that the course design and nature of the student sample may well influence the respondents' ability to identify three distinct dimensions of teaching presence, it is clear that more research is required. One suggested approach to studying this problem is to use a qualitative approach to gain insight into the students' perspectives (Diaz et al., 2010). Qualitative perspectives could also be useful to understand the role of social presence with regard to teaching and cognitive presence (Diaz et al., 2010). That is, why do students view social presence as more of a mediating variable (Garrison et al., 2010; Shea & Bidjerano, 2009a) and less important that the other presences (Diaz et al., 2010)? It may be useful to observe that we should not abandon qualitative approaches as we develop quantitative instruments such as the CoI survey. Qualitative approaches can provide insights and explanations not possible with objective instruments.

CoI Survey

Work to develop a quantitative instrument to measure the elements of the Community of Inquiry theoretical framework has been underway for the last few years. This reflects a need to address the inherent limitations of transcript analysis in terms of time and reliability while offering increased methodological possibilities and rigor. As noted in Chapter 2, recent studies across institutions have provided factor structure validation of the CoI theoretical framework and the associated survey instrument. The validation of the CoI survey represents a significant shift in the CoI research and opens up any number of possibilities for studies across institutions, disciplines, demographic groups, and technologies.

The CoI survey also provides the means and rigor to address "the need for conceptual refinement of the relationships and interactions between/among the elements, both particularly and collectively" (Garrison & Arbaugh, 2007, p. 165). Another area of future research lies in refining some of the survey items, particularly with regard to teaching presence. While the teaching presence construct remains strong, work may be needed to refine some of the items (Arbaugh, Cleveland-Innes, Diaz, Garrison, Ice, Richardson, Shea & Swan, 2008; Diaz et al., 2010). Finally, from a more pragmatic perspective preliminary work is being done to construct a short version that could be used for formative diagnostic purposes. Such an instrument could be of value to practitioners to assess the development of a community of learners.

The CoI survey instrument could also be a useful tool to study disciplinary differences. It is suggested that this research use the academic discipline framework reported in Arbaugh, Bangert & Cleveland-Innes (2010) to study subject matter effects on student perceptions across the elements of a community of inquiry. One area that needs further study is the congruence of the CoI theoretical framework that is based on a collaborative constructivist philosophy for "hard, pure disciplines" associated with direct instruction (Arbaugh et al., 2010, p. 43). We need to know whether cognitive presence effect is due to differences in discipline or more subtle teaching presence effects such as design and leadership approaches (Garrison et al., 2010). For example, a study that showed discipline differences with regard to approaches to learning appeared to be due to teaching presence (Garrison & Cleveland-Innes, 2005). A related area of research is to look at disciplines that approach their subject matter from an inductive or deductive perspective using the PI model; this might apply to the pure, soft social sciences in making sense of ill-structured content, and the applied, hard sciences in solving specific problems. Regardless, the CoI theory provides a coherent framework to explore disciplinary effects and opens up any number of research topics and hypotheses.

Lastly, a potentially productive area of research with great relevance in higher education is blended learning. The CoI theoretical framework has been used to understand the properties of face-to-face and online learning approaches. The CoI survey can again be an enormously valuable tool to study modes of communication across disciplines and technologies (Garrison & Vaughan, 2008). When and with what subject matter is it advantageous to use direct or mediated communication to create or sustain a community of inquiry?

Methodology

It is suggested that one of the reasons for the quick uptake and success of the CoI theoretical framework was the accompanying methodology. This methodology was used to analyze transcripts of online communities of inquiry. Notwithstanding the issues around questions such as which unit of analysis to use and what coding should be negotiated (Garrison, Cleveland-Innes, Koole & Kappelman, 2006), this methodology was instrumental in understanding the elements and dynamics of an online community of inquiry. This could be described as the exploratory and descriptive phase of research into e-learning. There was, however, a need for a quantitative research approach to move toward a more rigorous level of study of the CoI framework and its validation as a comprehensive theory of e-learning. This shift was marked by the development of the CoI survey and the initiation of large-scale empirical studies that provided predictive analyses and increased explanatory power.

In summary, it is a testament to the power of the CoI theoretical framework that it continues to spawn so many interesting and important research questions and potential hypotheses associated with e-learning. At the heart of this work is the goal of increasing our understanding of the composition and interaction of the three presences in creating and sustaining a community of inquiry that will support deep and meaningful e-learning approaches and learning outcomes. It is also important to explore the dimensionality of each of the presences and order of importance in the development of a community of inquiry.

Much research and development is required to realize the full potential of the CoI theoretical framework to create and sustain e-learning environments. This, however, does not take away from the CoI and its current value and potential as a theoretical framework.

CONCLUSION

As we shift from a focus on the gee whiz factor of technology and amusing but trivial applications, the resisters to educational change will come on side. Serious educators will recognize the potential of new and emerging communications technology and that education is about community, discourse, and reflection. There is a growing consensus that the *status quo* in the form of passive transmission of information is no longer relevant or acceptable. We are beginning to recognize that collaborative instructional designs using new and emerging communications technology are the means to a more meaningful and satisfying educational experience.

The great potential of e-learning in higher education is the restoration of community and critical discourse. The lasting capability of e-learning is to integrate both the breadth of the Web and the depth of discourse into an educational experience. Blended learning as framed here combines the breadth of access to information with the depth of discourse and reflection made possible by online communities of inquiry. However, this is predicated upon a progression from our fixation on access to information and social interaction to using technology to create worthwhile communities of inquiry. The emerging role and responsibility of educational institutions and educational leaders is to model and facilitate the potential of learning communities that restore the ideals of a traditional higher educational experience.

What is needed now in higher education is innovation and transformation. Not just technological innovation but educational innovation that can provide both the breadth of access and depth of community. We must recognize the space–time shift that e-learning represents. E-learning has the ability to eliminate boundaries and bring educational participants together in communities of inquiry. An e-learning community is where all participants are engaged in constructing meaning, collaboratively confirming understanding, and sharing knowledge. However, in the final analysis much work remains to confirm the multidimensional and dynamic elements of the CoI theoretical framework through rigorous studies. Certainly more work is required to shore up the theoretical foundation (Jezegou, 2010). Hopefully this book will serve as an inspiration and guide to address this need for theoretical and empirical studies and the growing interest in the practical implications of this framework.

E-learning has gained a foothold in higher education through the adoption of blended approaches to learning. E-learning in a blended context has come of age and will continue to grow this decade. It is inevitable that these developments will transform higher education through evolutionary processes. Mainstream distance education is still struggling with its adoption with a mass delivery model; however, e-learning in a distance education context has had pockets of growth and acceptance. Traditional higher education institutions are evolving to offer a range of e-learning choices among various forms of blended learning that capitalizes on the strengths of face-to-face and fully online experiences. Pure face-to-face courses without some form of e-learning experience are rapidly becoming an anomaly.

In the final analysis, technological innovation can dazzle but does not directly reveal educationally worthwhile outcomes. Educators are moving beyond the myth and hype of technology and are trying to figure out where we need to go educationally in a creative knowledge society. Higher education has reached the threshold of a new era that will see the convergence of pedagogical ideals and technological possibilities. The result will be the transformation of higher education.

Appendix

Developing a Community of Inquiry Instrument: Testing a Measure of the Community of Inquiry Framework using a Multi-institutional Sample

J.B. Arbaugh (a), Martha Cleveland-Innes (b), Sebastian R. Diaz (c), D. Randy Garrison (d), Philip Ice (e), Jennifer C. Richardson (f), Karen P. Swan (g)

a   College of Business, University of Wisconsin Oshkosh, 800 Algoma Blvd., Oshkosh, WI 54901, United States
b   Athabasca University, Canada
c   West Virginia University, United States
d   University of Calgary, Canada
e   American Public University System, United States
f   Purdue University, United States
g   Kent State University, United States

1. Introduction

With at least 356 citations to date (Google Scholar, May 2008), Garrison, Anderson and Archer (2000) Community of Inquiry (CoI) framework is becoming increasingly influential for explaining and prescribing the effective conduct of online learning. However, as long as there are no valid and reliable measures to test the framework, its impact to influence online learning theory will be limited. While the CoI framework has been examined extensively in qualitative studies (Anagnostopoulos, Basmadjian, & McCrory, 2005; Garrison & Cleveland- Innes, 2005; Oriogun, Ravenscroft, & Cook, 2005; Schrire, 2004), and individual components of the framework have been examined empirically (Richardson & Swan, 2003; Shea, Fredericksen, Pickett, & Pelz, 2003; Wise, Chang, Duffy, & del Valle, 2004), the number of studies that simultaneously examine all components of the framework empirically is extremely limited (Arbaugh, 2007; Garrison, Cleveland-Innes, & Fung, 2004). This concern has been noted recently by several scholars (Arbaugh, 2007; Garrison, 2007; Garrison & Arbaugh, 2007; Ho & Swan, 2007), and work to develop measures of the framework is underway.

However, the fact that these initial verification studies were conducted using single-institution samples limits their generalizability.

This article attempts to address these concerns by reporting on the development and testing of an instrument to measure the CoI framework using a multi-institutional sample. In addressing calls for a more quantitative orientation to research on the CoI and for more efficient measures of the framework (Arbaugh, 2007; Garrison, 2007; Ho & Swan, 2007), it is hoped that the measure of this framework that emerged from this study subsequently can be used to help researchers examine the relationship of the CoI to variables such as course outcomes (Shea, Li, & Pickett, 2006).

The rest of the article is organized as follows. Because the Internet and Higher Education has given extensive coverage to the CoI framework in previous articles (i.e. Arbaugh & Hwang, 2006; Garrison et al., 2000; Goertzen & Kristjansson, 2007; Shea et al., 2006; Vaughan & Garrison, 2005), the first section provides a brief overview of the framework. The second section of the article discusses the methods and results of testing a 34-item instrument. The article's final section discusses these findings and identifies potential implications for future research.

2. The Community of Inquiry Framework— an Overview

The CoI framework was first proposed to guide research into online learning (Garrison et al., 2000). It provided a collaborative-constructivist perspective to understanding the dynamics of an online learning experience. This is consistent with the traditional values of higher education to support discourse and reflection in a community of inquiry.

The catalyst for the generation of the CoI framework was the focus on social presence in the early days of exploring computer conferencing.

The identified need at that time was a comprehensive view of a formal online educational experience. The solution was to propose three overlapping presences—social, cognitive and teaching—that were highly interdependent (Garrison et al., 2000). At the heart of the overlap of these elements was a deep and meaningful educational experience.

Notwithstanding the order provided by the CoI framework, perhaps the main reason that the framework was widely adopted is the methodological guidelines for measuring each of the presences that constituted a community of inquiry. The first of these presences that required rigorous definition and operational rigor was social presence. Extending the original socio-emotional perspective, social presence is most recently defined as "the ability of participants to identify with the community (e.g., course of study), communicate purposefully in a trusting environment, and develop inter-personal relationships by way of projecting their individual personalities" (Garrison, 2009). From a methodological perspective, the three categories of social presence (open communication, group cohesion and personal/affective projection) are used to operationalize the concept.

The original definition of cognitive presence has been the most stable. It was defined by the Practical Inquiry Model consisting of four phases —triggering event, exploration, integration and resolution/application (Garrison, Anderson, & Archer, 2001). As such, cognitive presence is reflective of the purposeful nature of collaborative knowledge construction inherent in constructivist educational experiences. Although there are a limited number of studies that have focused on cognitive presence using this model, the model has been successful in measuring the developmental nature of the learning process across disciplines.

Teaching presence has been shown to be crucial in the satisfaction and success of a formal educational community of inquiry (Garrison & Arbaugh, 2007). Very much like the other presences, teaching presence is multi-dimensional and consists of three areas of responsibility—design, facilitation and direct instruction. Each of these is associated with the integration of social and cognitive processes in terms of the purposeful nature of the learning experience. The literature suggests that quantitative methodological techniques are required to validate the structure of teaching presence (Garrison & Arbaugh, 2007).

This framework has been used in a large number of studies, although most have followed the original methodology of analyzing transcripts. This exploratory, interpretivist approach certainly has shown to be fruitful, but it may be time to move from a descriptive to an inferential approach to studying online communities of inquiry. This would permit large studies of online and blended learning across institutions and disciplines. For this to happen we need to develop a structurally valid and psychometrically sound survey instrument with the potential to expand the study of online and blended learning. Such an instrument would also provide the means to study the structure of each of the presences and their inter-relationships.

3. Method and Results

The 34-item Community of Inquiry framework survey instrument was administered at four institutions in the Summer of 2007. Participating institutions were located in the United States and Canada. Participants in the study were enrolled in graduate-level courses in either Education or Business. 287 students volunteered to complete the survey, yielding a response rate of 43%.

Ordinal responses were scored using the scale (0=Strongly Disagree) to (4=Strongly Agree). Mean responses for the 34 items ranged from 2.90 for Item 16 (Online or web-based communication is an excellent medium for social interaction) to 3.63 for Item 4 (The instructor clearly communicated

Table A.1 Eigenvalues from Principal Component Analysis

Component	Initial eigenvalues			
	Total	% of variance	Cumulative %	Total
1	17.382	51.124	51.124	17.382
2	1.923	5.656	56.781	1.923
3	1.527	4.490	61.270	1.527
4	1.181	3.474	64.744	1.181

important due dates/time frames for learning activities). Standard deviations were highest for Item 16 (SD=1.04), and lowest for Item 1 (SD=0.66) (The instructor clearly communicated important course topics). When considering all respondents' ratings, teaching presence items collectively yield a mean score of 3.34 (SD=0.61). Social presence items collectively yield a mean score of 3.18 (SD=0.65), and cognitive presence items yield a mean score of 3.31 (SD=0.60).

The Principal Components Analysis (PCA) approach in SPSS version 15.0 was used to verify the three subscale structure of the 34 items comprising the CoI inventory. PCA was chosen to conform with two conditions of the study. First, development of the cognitive presence subscale required significantly more additions than the teaching and social presence subscales. Given the relative newness of the cognitive presence subscale, suggestions by Gorsuch (1983) and Thompson (2004) were applied and a more conservative exploratory approach to analysis was utilized. Second, PCA allowed for a more comprehensive analysis of variance, revealing significant detail related to the nature of the factors (Tabachnik & Fidell, 2007).

Assuming some degree of association among teaching, social, and cognitive presence (Garrison et al., 2004; Heckman & Annabi, 2005), oblique rotation (Direct Obliminal in SPSS) was utilized with the default value δ=0 specified to limit reasonably the level of correlation among the factors. The use of an oblique rotation was justified on theoretical grounds that the three presences were considered to be interdependent.

The sample size (n=287) for this study is reasonably adequate depending on the rule of thumb utilized. The study meets Kass and Tinsley's (1979) recommendation for 5 to 10 participants per item, yet fails to meet other recommendations of at least 10 or more respondents per item (Nunnally, 1978). Some authors suggest absolute sample sizes of n=300 being adequate (Tabachnik & Fidell, 2007). More specifically, Comrey and Lee (1992) rate sample sizes of 200 as Fair and 300 as Good.

The Keyser–Meyer–Olkin (KMO) measure of sampling adequacy is 0.96, suggesting factor analysis should yield distinct and reliable factors given the data utilized. Respective KMO values for individual items are all very good, ranging from 0.921 to 0.983.

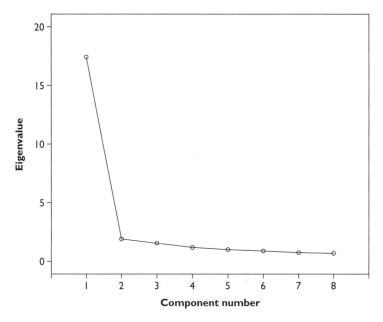

Figure A.1 Resuls of Scree Test

Table A.1 and Figure A.1 show the eigenvalues and the scree plot for our principal components analysis. When specifying a three-factor solution within SPSS, factor loadings for the 34 items support the validity of the CoI's conceptual framework of Teaching, Social, and Cognitive Presences. These three factors accounted for 61.3% of the total variance in scores. Principal Components Analysis did yield an additional fourth factor with an eigenvalue N1.0. However, the respective scree plot fails to inform the possibility of an additional fourth factor given the marked decrease in magnitude of the first and second factor's eigenvalues. Over half (51.1%) the total variance in this three-factor solution is attributed to the first factor.

Table A.2 lists for the 34 CoI items factor loadings on each of the three factors. These results reflect the Pattern Matrix generated by SPSS.

Although factor loadings for the respective Structure Matrix differ slightly, results from both output matrices support the three-factor model. Consistent with the design of the instrument, Items 1–13 (teaching presence) loaded most heavily on Factor 1. Items 14–22 (social presence) loaded most heavily on Factor 2. Finally, Items 23–34 (cognitive presence) loaded most heavily on Factor 3. Cronbach's Alpha yielded internal consistencies equal to 0.94 for teaching presence, 0.91 for social presence, and 0.95 for cognitive presence.

Table A.2 Pattern Matrix

Pattern matrix[a]	Component		
	1	2	3
1 The instructor clearly communicated important course topics	**0.826**	0.088	0.067
2 The instructor clearly communicated important course goals	**0.877**	−0.021	0.046
3 The instructor provided clear instructions on how to participate in course learning activities	**0.592**	0.246	−0.035
4 The instructor clearly communicated important due dates/time frames for learning activities	**0.611**	0.078	0.040
5 The instructor was helpful in identifying areas of agreement and disagreement on course topics that helped me to learn	**0.579**	0.162	−0.138
6 The instructor was helpful in guiding the class towards understanding course topics in a way that helped me clarify my thinking	**0.575**	0.091	−0.281
7 The instructor helped to keep course participants engaged and participating in productive dialogue	**0.633**	0.149	−0.160
8 The instructor helped keep the course participants on task in a way that helped me to learn	**0.579**	0.042	−0.285
9 The instructor encouraged course participants to explore new concepts in this course	**0.523**	0.099	−0.233
10 Instructor actions reinforced the development of a sense of community among course participants	**0.569**	0.174	−0.176
11 The instructor helped to focus discussion on relevant issues in a way that helped me to learn	**0.425**	0.146	−0.374
12 The instructor provided feedback that helped me understand my strengths and weaknesses relative to the course's goals and objectives	**0.649**	−0.123	−0.201
13 The instructor provided feedback in a timely fashion	**0.513**	−0.025	−0.103
14 Getting to know other course participants gave me a sense of belonging in the course	0.050	**0.619**	−0.233
15 I was able to form distinct impressions of some course participants	0.172	**0.473**	0.013
16 Online or web-based communication is an excellent medium for social interaction	−0.181	**0.674**	−0.226
17 I felt comfortable conversing through the online medium	−0.039	**0.814**	0.015
18 I felt comfortable participating in the course discussions	0.109	**0.788**	0.005
19 I felt comfortable interacting with other course participants	0.286	**0.701**	0.038
20 I felt comfortable disagreeing with other course participants while still maintaining a sense of trust	0.103	**0.620**	−0.034
21 I felt that my point of view was acknowledged by other course participants	0.319	**0.556**	0.025

22	Online discussions help me to develop a sense of collaboration	0.047	**0.561**	−0.340
23	Problems posed increased my interest in course issues	−0.099	0.172	**−0.785**
24	Course activities piqued my curiosity	0.064	0.070	**−0.712**
25	I felt motivated to explore content related questions	0.082	−0.031	**−0.770**
26	I utilized a variety of information sources to explore problems posed in this course	0.078	−0.158	**−0.759**
27	Brainstorming and finding relevant information helped me resolve content-related questions	−0.106	0.130	**−0.794**
28	Online discussions were valuable in helping me appreciate different perspectives	−0.096	0.286	**−0.699**
29	Combining new information helped me answer questions raised in course activities	0.101	0.043	**−0.716**
30	Learning activities helped me construct explanations/solutions	0.128	0.030	**−0.732**
31	Reflection on course content and discussion helped me understand fundamental concepts in this class	0.008	0.237	**−0.640**
32	I can describe ways to test and apply the knowledge created in this course	0.239	−0.097	**−0.619**
33	I have developed solutions to course problems that can be applied in practice	0.147	0.026	**−0.653**
34	I can apply the knowledge created in this course to my work or other non-class related activities	0.171	−0.041	**−0.687**

Rotation method: Oblimin with Kaiser Normalization. Survey items that loaded on a component at .5 or higher are in bold.

[a] Rotation converged in 12 iterations.

4. Discussion

The Principal Components Analysis of the data supports the construct validity of teaching presence, social presence, and cognitive presence as measured by the CoI. However, when allowing for any possible number of factors in the analysis, eigenvalues indicate a potential fourth factor, while the scree plot yields inconclusive results.

The factor loadings are consistent with recent studies that suggest a two-dimensional orientation of items used to measure teaching presence. Studies by both Arbaugh (2007) and Shea et al. (2006) have found that pre-course activities (design and organization) and in-course activities (facilitation and direct instruction) load on separate factors. Arbaugh (2007) suggested that this loading may reflect the time orientation during which these activities take place. Since most of the activities related to design and organization take place before the course begins, and facilitation and instruction are activities that take place during the course, it is possible that the timing of activities influences the operationalization of the framework.

The results of this study support the use of the CoI instrument as a valid measure of teaching, social, and cognitive presence. As subsequent research is conducted with the CoI, investigators in this study hope to explore further the inconsistencies between factor analysis results and the intended structure of CoI items when the number of factors is not specified a priori. These inconsistencies may simply result from subtleties in how particular items are worded. On the other hand, such inconsistencies may point to more fundamental issues regarding theoretical assumptions on which the subscale items are created.

Comparisons among the factor loadings lend support that in some instances, the wording of CoI items measuring teaching presence may simply need to be refined slightly. For example, with Items 1 and 12, the primary factor loadings are not as distinct. That is, they are not as dissimilar from the next highest loading as compared to other items. These loadings suggest that overall such items do not factor out "as cleanly," and may thus be due to vagueness in how they are worded.

Results also point to other problems with the items comprising teaching presence. Correlations among the four factors obtained when not specifying a factor solution, illustrated in Table A.3, suggest that Factor 1, comprised of seven of the 13 items designed to measure teaching presence, is more highly correlated with the cognitive presence factor ($r=-0.479$) than it is with the factor containing the remainder of teaching presence items ($r=0.348$). If Factors 1 and 4 were more closely correlated, one would suspect less that a separate construct actually exists. However, these results suggest that given respondents' perceptions, items comprising teaching presence might measure two distinct constructs.

It is important to distinguish, however, the validity of the teaching presence construct per se, and the validity of the items designed to measure that construct. That is, in keeping with not "throwing the baby out with the bathwater," CoI items used to measure teaching presence may need to be refined, yet the theoretical basis of the construct itself remains intact based on the valuable work conducted in this area. Moreover, as alluded to above, construct validity is highly dependent on the context in which measurement occurs. For example, were these teaching presence items administered to respondents independent of the remaining items for social and cognitive

Table A.3 Correlations Between Components

Component	1	2	3	4
1	1.000	0.318	−0.479	0.348
2	0.318	1.000	−0.568	0.382
3	−0.479	−0.568	1.000	−0.543
4	0.348	0.382	−0.543	1.000

presence, respondents' perceptions of those items may be markedly different. In attempting to merge three separate constructs into one instrument, investigators assume the risk of unintentionally creating new and complex phenomena resulting from the interactions among the three constructs. In fact, the results of this study suggest there is such overlap, as evidenced by correlation among factors. Furthermore, when considering the sample of respondents, investigators need to anticipate that, rather than take a survey at face value, students possessing higher cognitive intelligence than the general population will invariably attempt to "decode" a survey as they complete it. In summary, one must consider carefully when attempting to validate an instrument to do so.

Another scenario needs to be considered when scrutinizing the teaching presence construct. Much as the more general construct of presence in an online learning environment can be explained more in depth by separating out teaching, social, and cognitive subfactors, it may be that the teaching presence construct's potential bifurcation reflects a strength, and not necessarily a weakness, in the subscale's construction. That is, since this factor represents a greater chunk of the total variance, results may simply be pointing to the teaching presence subscale itself having two or more subscales. At this early stage of development of measures to operationalize the CoI framework it is important not to assume that a subscale's multidimensionality is necessarily a weakness. Further studies conducted with larger samples and within other contexts will help clarify this issue.

In spite of potential concerns with the conceptualization of teaching presence, the results of this study suggest that this attempt to operationalize the CoI framework builds upon prior work in at least two ways. First, the survey items measuring cognitive presence appear to capture the dimensions of that construct in a valid yet efficient manner. Second, the multi-institutional sample provides increased external validity to the findings. As such, the instrument could be used both in studies that examine the CoI elements as predictor variables of course outcomes and as criterion variables in studies examining the extent to which course characteristics encourage or inhibit the development of social, teaching, and/or cognitive presence. We encourage other researchers to work to further refine these measures.

We also encourage exploratory works that use the CoI as a dependent measure in comparing courses and the implementation of emerging technologies within courses. Initial work in this area indicates that the CoI may be quite effective in determining the impact of specific strategies and technologies (Ice, 2008). Further experimental or quasi-experimental studies of this nature would be of significant benefit in defining best practices in online environments.

The increasing reliability and validity of CoI measurements carries implications not only for researchers interested in the framework, but also for course designers, degree program administrators, and instructors. As CoI measures are further refined, should they be used as a course and program assessment tool in addition to research purposes? Also, regardless of the definition of the construct of teaching presence, our findings suggest that instructors play significant roles both in helping students understand and apply appropriate conduct within the course before it begins and in guiding the course activities once the course is underway.

References

Anagnostopoulos, D., Basmadjian, K. G., & McCrory, R. S. (2005). The decentered teacher and the construction of social space in the virtual classroom. *Teachers College Record*, 107, 1699–1729.

Arbaugh, J. B. (2007). An empirical verification of the community of inquiry framework. *Journal of Asynchronous Learning Networks*, 11(1), 73–85.

Arbaugh, J. B., & Hwang, A. (2006). Does "teaching presence" exist in online MBA courses? *The Internet and Higher Education*, 9, 9–21.

Comrey, A. L., & Lee, H. B. (1992). *A first course in factor analysis*. Hillsdale, NJ: Erlbaum.

Garrison, D. R. (2007). Online community of inquiry review: Social, cognitive, and teaching presence issues. *Journal of Asynchronous Learning Networks*, 11(1), 61–72.

Garrison, D. R. (2009). Communities of inquiry in online learning: Social, teaching and cognitive presence. In P. L. Rogers et al. (Eds.), *Encyclopedia of distance learning*, 2nd Edition (pp. 352–355). Hershey, PA: IGI Global.

Garrison, D. R., Anderson, T., & Archer, W. (2000). Critical inquiry in a text-based environment: Computer conferencing in higher education. *The Internet and Higher Education*, 2, 87–105.

Garrison, D. R., Anderson, T., & Archer, W. (2001). Critical thinking, cognitive presence, and computer conferencing in distance education. *American Journal of Distance Education*, 15(1), 7–23.

Garrison, D. R., & Arbaugh, J. B. (2007). Researching the Community of Inquiry Framework: Review, issues and future directions. *The Internet and Higher Education*, 10(3), 157–172.

Garrison, D. R., & Cleveland-Innes, M. (2005). Facilitating cognitive presence in online learning: Interaction is not enough. *American Journal of Distance Education*, 19, 133–148.

Garrison, D. R., Cleveland-Innes, M., & Fung, T. (2004). Student role adjustment in online communities of inquiry: Model and instrument validation. *Journal of Asynchronous Learning Networks*, 8(2). Retrieved September 1, 2004 from http://www.aln.org/publications/jaln/v8n2/v8n2_garrison.asp.

Goertzen, P., & Kristjansson, C. (2007). Interpersonal dimensions of community in graduate online learning: Exploring social presence through the lens of Systemic Functional Linguistics. *The Internet and Higher Education*, 10, 212–230.

Gorsuch, R. (1983). *Factor analysis*, 2nd Edition. Hillsdale, NJ: Lawrence Erlbaum.

Heckman, R., & Annabi, H. (2005). A content analytic comparison of learning processes in online and face-to-face case study discussions. *Journal of Computer-*

Mediated Communication, 10(2) article 7. http://jcmc.indiana.edu/vol10/issue2/heckman.html.

Ho, C.-H., & Swan, K. (2007). Evaluating online conversation in an asynchronous learning environment: An application of Grice's cooperative principle. *The Internet and Higher Education*, 10, 3–14.

Ice, P. (April, 2008). The impact of asynchronous audio feedback on teaching, social and cognitive presence. Banff, Alberta: First International Conference of the Canadian Network for Innovation in Education.

Kass, R. A., & Tinsley, H. E. A. (1979). Factor analysis. *Journal of Leisure Research*, 11, 120–138.

Nunnally, J. C. (1978). *Psychometric theory*, 2nd Edition. New York: McGraw-Hill.

Oriogun, P. K., Ravenscroft, A., & Cook, J. (2005). Validating an approach to examining cognitive engagement in online groups. *American Journal of Distance Education*, 19, 197–214.

Richardson, J. C., & Swan, K. (2003). Examining social presence in online courses in relation to students' perceived learning and satisfaction. *Journal of Asynchronous Learning Networks*, 7(1). Retrieved June 1, 2004 from: http://www.aln.org/publications/jaln/v7n1/index.asp.

Schrire, S. (2004). Interaction and cognition in asynchronous computer conferencing. *Instructional Science: An International Journal of Learning and Cognition*, 32, 475–502.

Shea, P. J., Fredericksen, E. E., Pickett, A. M., & Pelz, W. E. (2003). A preliminary investigation of "teaching presence" in the SUNY learning network. In J. Bourne & Janet C. Moore (Eds.), *Elements of quality online education into the mainstream*, Vol. 4 (pp. 279–312). Needham, MA: Sloan-C.

Shea, P., Li, C. S., & Pickett, A. (2006). A study of teaching presence and student sense of learning community in fully online and web-enhanced college courses. *The Internet and Higher Education*, 9, 175–190.

Tabachnik, B. G., & Fidell, L. S. (2007). *Using multivariate statistics*. Boston: Pearson Education.

Thompson, B. (2004). *Exploratory and confirmatory factor analysis: Understanding concepts and applications*. Washington, DC: American Psychological Association.

Vaughan, N., & Garrison, D. R. (2005). Creating cognitive presence in a blended faculty development community. *The Internet and Higher Education*, 8, 1–12.

Wise, A., Chang, J., Duffy, T., & del Valle, R. (2004). The effects of teacher social presence on student satisfaction, engagement, & learning. *Journal of Educational Computing Research*, 31, 247–271.

References

Achenbach, J. (1999). The too-much-information age. *The Washington Post*, March 12, A23.

Akyol, Z., Arbaugh, J. B., Cleveland-Innes, M., Garrison, D. R., Ice, P., Richardson, J. & Swan, K. (2009). A response to the review of the community of inquiry framework. *Journal of Distance Education*, 23(2), 123–136.

Akyol, Z. & Garrison, D. R. (2008). The development of a community of inquiry over time in an online course: Understanding the progression and integration of social, cognitive and teaching presence. *Journal of Asynchronous Learning Networks*, 12(3), 3–22.

Akyol, Z. & Garrison, D. R. (in press a). Understanding cognitive presence in an online and blended community of inquiry: Assessing outcomes and processes for deep approaches to learning. *British Journal of Educational Technology*.

Akyol, Z. & Garrison, D. R. (in press b). Learning and satisfaction in online communities of inquiry. In S. Eom & J. B. Arbaugh (Eds.), *Student satisfaction and learning outcomes in e-learning: An introduction to empirical research*. Hershey, PA: IGI Global.

Akyol, Z. & Garrison, D. R. (unpublished). Assessing metacognition in an online community of inquiry.

Akyol, Z., Garrison, D. R. & Ozden, M. Y. (2009). Online and blended communities of inquiry: Exploring the developmental and perceptual differences. *International Review of Research in Open and Distance Learning*, 10(6), 65–83.

Akyol, Z., Ice, P., Garrison, D. R. & Mitchell, R. (2010). The relationship between course socio-epistemological orientations and student perceptions of community of inquiry. *Internet and Higher Education*, 13(1–2), 66–68.

An, H., Shin, S. & Lim, K. (2009). The effects of different instructor facilitation approaches on students' interactions during asynchronous online discussions. *Computers & Education*, 53, 749–760.

Anderson, T. (2001). The hidden curriculum of distance education. *Change Magazine*, 33(6), 29–35.

Anderson, T. & Mason, R. (1993). The Bangkok Project: New tool for professional development. *American Journal of Distance Education*, 7(2), 5–18.

Anderson, T., Rourke, L., Garrison, D. R. & Archer, W. (2001). Assessing teacher presence in a computer conferencing context. *Journal of Asynchronous Learning Networks*, 5(2), 1–17.

Arbaugh, J. B., Bangert, A. & Cleveland-Innes, M. (2010). Subject matter effects and the Community of Inquiry (CoI) framework: An exploratory study. *Internet and Higher Education*, 13(1–2), 37–44.

Arbaugh, J. B. & Benbunan-Fich, R. (2006). An investigation of epistemological and social dimensions of teaching in online learning environments. *Academy of Management Learning & Education*, 5(4), 435–447.

Arbaugh, J. B., Cleveland-Innes, M., Diaz, S., Garrison, D. R., Ice, P., Richardson, J. Shea, P. & Swan, K. (2008). Developing a community of inquiry instrument: Testing a measure of the Community of Inquiry framework using a multi-institutional sample. *Internet and Higher Education*, 11, 133–136.

Archer, W. (2010). Beyond online discussions: Extending the community of inquiry framework to entire courses. *Internet and Higher Education*, 13, 69.

Archer, W., Garrison, D. R. and Anderson, T. (1999). Adopting disruptive technologies in traditional universities: Continuing education as an incubator for innovation. *Canadian Journal of University Continuing Education*, 25(1), 13–30.

Baker, J. D. (2004). An investigation of relationships among instructor immediacy and affective and cognitive learning in the online classroom. *Internet and Higher Education*, 7(1), 1–13.

Bangert, A. (2008). The influence of social and teaching presence on the quality of online critical inquiry. *Journal of Computing in Higher Education*, 20(1), 34–61.

Benbunan-Fich, R. & Arbaugh, J. B. (2006). Separating the effects of knowledge construction and group collaboration in learning outcomes of web-based courses. *Information & Management*, 43(6), 778–793.

Bereiter, C. (1992). Referent-centred and problem-centred knowledge: Elements of an educational epistemology. *Interchange*, 23, 337–361.

Biggs, J. B. (1987). *Student approaches to learning and studying*. Melbourne, Australia: Australian Council for Educational Research.

Blanchette, J. (2001). Questions in the online learning environment. *Journal of Distance Education*, 16(2), 37–57.

Bliss, C. A. & Lawrence, B. (2009). From posts to patterns: A metric to characterize discussion board activity in online courses. *Journal of Asynchronous Learning Networks*, 13(2), 15–32.

Brook, C. & Oliver, R. (2007). Exploring the influence of instructor actions on community development in online settings. In N. Lambropoulos & P. Zaphiris (Eds.), *User-centered design of online learning communities*. Hersey: Idea Group.

Boston, W., Diaz, S. R., Gibson, A., Ice, P., Richardson, J. & Swan, K. (2009). An exploration of the relationship between indicators of the community of inquiry framework and retention in online programs. *Journal of Asynchronous Learning Networks*, 13(3), 67–83.

Brown, J. S. & Adler, R. P. (2008). Minds on fire: Open education, the long tail, and learning 2.0. *EDUCAUSE Review*, 43(1), 16–32.

Brown, M. B. & Diaz, V. (2010). *Mobile learning: Context and prospects. A report on the ELI focus session*. ELI Paper 1, EDUCAUSE.

Brown, R. E. (2001). The process of community-building in distance learning classes. *Journal of Asynchronous Learning Networks*, 5(2), 18–35.

Buraphadeja, V. & Dawson, K. (2008). Content analysis in Computer-mediated communication: Analyzing models for assessing critical thinking through the lens of social constructivism. *American Journal of Distance Education*, 22(3), 130–145.

Burbules, N. (1993). *Dialogue in teaching: Theory and practice.* New York: Teachers College Press.

Caspi, A. & Blau, I. (2008). Social presence in online discussion groups: testing three conceptions and their relations to perceived learning. *Social Psychology of Education,* 11(3), 323–346.

Cecez-Kecmanovic, D. & Webb, C. (2000). Towards a communicative model of collaborative web-mediated learning. *Australian Journal of Educational Technology,* 16(1), 73–85.

Chapman, C., Ramondt, L. & Smiley, G. (2005). Strong community, deep learning: Exploring the link. *Innovations in Education and Teaching International,* 42(3), 217–230.

Christensen, C. (1997). *The Innovator's dilemma: When new technologies cause great firms to fail.* Boston: Harvard Business School Press.

Clark, B. R. (1998). *Creating entrepreneurial universities: Organizational pathways of transformation.* Guildford, UK: Pergamon.

Clark, R. E. (1983). Reconsidering research on learning from media. *Review of Educational Research,* 53, 445–459.

Clark, R. (1994). Media will never influence learning. *Educational Technology Research and Development,* 42(3), 21–29.

Cleveland-Innes, M. & Garrison, D. R. (Eds.) (2010). *An introduction to distance education: Understanding teaching and learning in a new era.* London: Routledge.

Cleveland-Innes, M., Garrison, D. R. & Kinsell, E. (2007). Role adjustment for learners in an online community of inquiry: Identifying the challenges of incoming online learners. *International Journal of Web-Based Learning and Teaching Technologies,* 2(1), 1–16.

Collison, G., Elbaum, B., Haavind, S. & Tinker, R. (2000). *Facilitating online learning: Effective strategies for moderators.* Madison, WI: Atwood Publishing.

Conrad, D. (2005). Building and maintaining community in cohort-based online learning. *Journal of Distance Education,* 20(1), 1–20.

Cotton, D. & Yorke, J. (2006). Analyzing online discussions: What are the students learning? In *Proceedings of the 23rd Annual Conference of the Australasian Society for Computers in Learning in Tertiary Education: "Who's learning? Whose technology?"* December, 2006, Sydney, Australia.

Davie, L. (1989). Facilitation techniques for the online tutor. In R. Mason & A. Kaye (Eds.), *MindWeave.* (pp. 74–85). Oxford: Pergamon Press.

de Leng, B. A., Dolmans, D. H. J. M., Jobsis, R., Muijtjens, A. M. M. & van der Vleuten, C. P. M. (2009). Exploration of an e-learning model to foster critical thinking on basic science concepts during work placements. *Computers & Education,* 53(1), 1–13.

Dewey, J. (1916). *Democracy and education.* New York: Macmillan.

Dewey, J. (1933). *How we think* (rev. edn.). Boston: D.C. Heath.

Dewey, J. (1938). *Experience and education.* New York: Collier Macmillan.

Dewey, J. (1967). Psychology. In J. A. Boydston (Ed.), *John Dewey: The early works, 1882–1898 Vol. 2* (pp. 204–213). Carbondale: Southern Illinois University Press. (Original work published 1887.)

Dewey, J. & Childs, J. L. (1981). The underlying philosophy of education. In J. A. Boydston (Ed.), *John Dewey: The later works, 1925–1953, Vol. 8* (pp. 77–103). Carbondale: Southern Illinois University Press. (Original work published 1933.)

Diaz, S. R., Swan, K., Ice, P. & Kupczynski, L. (2010). Stu[...] importance of survey items, multiplicative factor analysis, an[...] community of inquiry survey. *Internet and Higher Education,*

Dubin, R. (1978). *Theory building* (2nd edn.). NY: The Free Press.

Duderstadt, J. J., Atkins, D. E. & Van Houweling, D. (2002). Hi[...] *the digital age: Technology issues and strategies for Americ[...]eges and universities.* Westport, CT: Greenwood Press.

Dziuban, C., Hartman, J., Moskal, P., Sorg, S. & Truman, B. (2004). Three ALN modalities: An institutional perspective. In J. Bourne & J. C. Moore (Eds.), *Elements of quality online education: Into the mainstream* (pp. 127–148). Needham, MA: Sloan-C.

ELI (2010). 7 things you should know about mobile apps for learning. Retrieved May 14, 2010 from http://www.educause.edu/Resources/7ThingsYouShouldKnow AboutMobil/204763.

E-learning in tertiary education: Where do we stand? (2005). Centre for Educational Research and Innovation, OECD Publishing. Retrieved July 28, 2010 from http://books.google.ca/books?id=8viUZBYLQysC&printsec=frontcover&dq=E-learning+in+tertiary+education:+Where+do+we+stand&source=bl&ots=2JkJ_99J bO&sig=eF7-9gJaIi-Px0EfuSGMUXI8-sE&hl=en&ei=Cs1RTI-QJM-EnQff3pS0Aw&sa=X&oi=book_result&ct=result&resnum=3&ved=0CB8Q6AE wAg#v=onepage&q&f=false.

Entwistle, N. J. & Ramsden, P. (1983). *Understanding student learning.* London: Croom Helm.

Evans, T. & Pauling, B. (2010). The future of distance education: Reformed, scrapped or recycled. In M. Cleveland-Innes & D. R. Garrison (Eds.), *An introduction to distance education: Understanding teaching and learning in a new era.* London: Routledge.

Fabro, K. R. & Garrison, D. R. (1998). Computer conferencing and higher-order learning. *Indian Journal of Open Learning,* 7(1), 41–54.

Feenberg, A. (1999). *Questioning technology.* London: Routledge.

Garrison, D. R. (1997a). Computer conferencing: The post-industrial age of distance education. *Open Learning,* 12(2), 3–11.

Garrison, D. R. (1997b). Self-directed learning: Toward a comprehensive model. *Adult Education Quarterly,* 48(1), 18–33.

Garrison, D. R. (2003). Cognitive presence for effective asynchronous online learning: The role of reflective inquiry, self-direction and metacognition. In J. Bourne & J. C. Moore (Eds.), *Elements of quality online education: Practice and direction* (pp. 29–38). Volume 4 in the Sloan C Series, Needham, MA: The Sloan Consortium.

Garrison, D. R. (2009a). Implications of online learning for the conceptual development and practice of distance education. *Journal of Distance Education,* 23(2), 93–104.

Garrison, D. R. (2009b). Communities of inquiry in online learning. In P. L. Rogers et al. (Eds.), *Encyclopedia of distance learning* (2nd edn.) (pp. 352–355). Hershey, PA: IGI Global.

Garrison, D. R. & Anderson, T. (1999). Avoiding the industrialization of research universities: Big and little distance education. *American Journal of Distance Education,* 13(2), 48–63.

Garrison, D. R., Anderson, T. & Archer, W. (2000). Critical inquiry in a text-based environment: Computer conferencing in higher education. *The Internet and Higher Education*, 2(2/3), 87–105.

Garrison, D. R., Anderson, T. & Archer, W. (2001). Critical thinking, cognitive presence and computer conferencing in distance education. *American Journal of Distance Education*, 15(1), 7–23.

Garrison, D. R. & Arbaugh, J. B. (2007). Researching the community of inquiry framework: Review, issues, and future directions. *Internet and Higher Education*, 10(3), 157–172.

Garrison, D. R. & Archer, W. (2000). *A transactional perspective on teaching and learning: A framework for adult and higher education*. Oxford, UK: Pergamon.

Garrison, D. R. & Cleveland-Innes, M. (2005). Facilitating cognitive presence in online learning: Interaction is not enough. *American Journal of Distance Education*, 19(3), 133–148.

Garrison, D. R. & Cleveland-Innes, M. (2010). Foundations of distance education. In M. Cleveland-Innes & D. R. Garrison (Eds.), *An introduction to distance education: Understanding teaching and learning in a new era*. London: Routledge.

Garrison, D. R., Cleveland-Innes, M. & Fung, T. S. (2010). Exploring causal relations among teaching, cognitive and social presence: A holistic view of the community of inquiry framework. *Internet and Higher Education*, 13(1–2), 31–36.

Garrison, D. R., Cleveland-Innes, M., Koole, M. & Kappelman, J. (2006). Revisiting methodological issues in the analysis of transcripts: Negotiated coding and reliability. *The Internet and Higher Education*, 9(1), 1–8.

Garrison, D. R. & Vaughan, N. (2008). *Blended learning in higher education*. San Francisco: Jossey-Bass.

Garrison, J. (1997). *Dewey and eros: Wisdom and desire in the art of teaching*. New York: Teachers College Press.

Gilbert, S. W. (2000). So, why bother? *AAHESGIT*, 49, Retrieved June 6, 2002 from http://www.tltgroup.org/whybother.htm.

Gladwell, M. (2002). *The tipping point: How little things can make a big difference*. NY: Little, Brown and Company.

Gorsky, P., Caspi, A., Antonovsky, A., Blau, I. & Mansur, A. (2010). The relationship between academic discipline and dialogic behaviour in open university course forums. *International Review of Research in Open and Distance Learning*, 11(2), 49–72.

Gorsky, P., Caspi, A. & Smidt, S. (2007). Use of instructional dialogue by university students in a difficult distance education physics course. *Journal of Distance Education*, 21(3), 1–22.

Green, R. (1998). *The forty-eight laws of power*. NY: Viking Press.

Gunawardena, C. N. (1991). Collaborative learning and group dynamics in computer-mediated communication networks. *Research Monograph of the American Center for the Study of Distance Education*, 9 (pp. 14–24). University Park, Pennsylvania: The Pennsylvania State University.

Gunawardena, C. N. (1995). Social presence theory and implication for interaction and collaborative learning in computer conferences. *International Journal of Educational telecommunications*, 1(2/3), 147–166.

Gunawardena, C. N. & Zittle, F. J. (1997). Social presence as a predictor of satisfaction within a computer-mediated conferencing environment. *The American Journal of Distance Education*, 11(3), 8–26.

Guri-Rosenblit, S. (2009). *Digital technologies in higher education: Sweeping expectations and actual effects.* New York: Nova Science Publishers.

Harasim, L. (1987). Teaching and learning on-line: Issues in computer-mediated graduate courses. *Canadian Journal of Educational Communication,* 16, 117–135.

Harasim, L. (1989). On-line education: A new domain. In R. Mason & A. R. Kaye (Eds.), *Mindweave: Communication, computers, and distance education* (pp. 50–62). New York: Pergamon.

Hartshorne, R. & Ajjan, H. (2009). Examining student decisions to adopt Web 2.0 technologies: Theory and empirical tests. *Journal of Computing in Higher Education,* 21, 183–198.

Harvey, D., Moller, L. A., Huett, J. B., Godshalk, V. M. & Downs, M. (2007). Identifying factors that effect learning community development and performance in asynchronous distance education. In R. Luppicini (Ed.), *Online learning communities* (pp. 169–187). N.C.: Information Age Publishing.

Hiltz, S. R. & Turoff, M. (1993). *The network nation: Human communication via computer.* Cambridge, MA: MIT Press.

Ice, P. (2010). The future of learning technologies: Transformational developments. In M. F. Cleveland-Innes & D. R. Garrison (Eds.), *Teaching and learning in distance education: Enter a new era.* London: Routledge.

Ice, P., Arbaugh, B., Diaz, S., Garrison, D. R., Richardson, J., Shea, P. & Swan, K. (2007). *Community of Inquiry framework: Validation and instrument development.* The 13th Annual Sloan-C International Conference on Online Learning, Orlando, November.

Ice, P., Curtis, R., Phillips, P. & Wells, J. (2007). Using asynchronous audio feedback to enhance teaching presence and students' sense of community. *Journal of Asynchronous Learning Networks,* 11(2), 3–25.

Ikenberry, S. O. (1999). The university and the information age. In W. Z. Hirsch & L. E. Weber (Eds.), *Challenges facing higher education at the millennium.* Phoenix, Arizona: Oryx Press.

Jahng, N., Nielsen, W. S. & Chan, E. K. H. (2010). Collaborative learning in an online course: A comparison of communication patterns in small and whole group activities. *Journal of Distance Education,* 24(2), 39–58.

Jezegou, A. (2010). Community of inquiry en e-learning: a propos du modele de Garrison et Anderson. *Journal of Distance Education,* 24(2), 1–18.

Jiang, M. & Ting, E. (2000). A study of factors influencing students' perceived learning in a web-based course environment. *International Journal of Educational Telecommunications,* 6(4), 317–338.

Johnson, D. W. & Johnson, R. T. (2009). An educational psychology success story: Social interdependence theory and cooperative learning. *Educational Researcher,* 38(5), 365–379.

Kang, K. M. & Kim, M. J. (2006). Investigation of the relationship among perceived social presence, achievement, satisfaction and learning persistence in the blended learning environment. *Journal of Educational Technology,* 22(4), 1–27.

Katz, R. N. (2010). Scholars, scholarship, and the scholarly enterprise in the digital age. *EDUCAUSE Review,* 45(2), 44–56.

Kaye, T. (1987). Introducing computer-mediated communication into a distance education system. *Canadian Journal of Educational Communication,* 16, 153–166.

Ke, F. (2010). Examining online teaching, cognitive, and social presence for adult students. *Computers & Education*, 55, 808–820.

Kim, J. (in press). Developing an instrument to measure social presence in distance higher education. *British Journal of Educational Technology*.

Koole, M., McQuilkin, J. L. & Ally, M. (2010). Mobile learning in distance education: Utility or futility? *Journal of Distance Education*, 24(2), 59–82.

Kozma, R. (1994). Will media influence learning? Reframing the debate. *Educational Technology Research & Development*, 42(2), 7–19.

Laumakis, M., Graham, C. & Dziuban, C. (2009). The Sloan-C pillars and boundary objects in framework for evaluating blended learning. *Journal of Asynchronous Learning Networks*, 13(1), 75–87.

Lim, D. H., Morris, M. L. & Kupritz, V. W. (2007). Online vs. blended learning: Differences in instructional outcomes and learner satisfaction. *Journal of Asynchronous Learning Networks*, 11(3), 27–42.

Liu, S., Gomez, J. & Yen, C. (2009). Community college online course retention and final grade: Predictability of social presence. *Journal of Interactive Online Learning*, 8(2), 165–182.

Liu, X., Magjuka, R. J., Bonk, C. J. & Lee, S. H. (2007). Does sense of community matter? An examination of participants' perceptions of building learning communities in online courses. *Quarterly Review of Distance Education*, 8(1), 9–24.

Lipman, M. (1991). *Thinking in education*. Cambridge: Cambridge University Press.

Lipman, M. (2003). *Thinking in education* (2nd edn.). Cambridge: Cambridge University Press.

Lombardi, M. M. (2008). *Making the grade: The role of assessment in authentic learning*. ELI Paper 1, EDUCAUSE. Retrieved July 29, 2010 from http://www.educause.edu/ELI/MakingtheGradeTheRoleofAssessm/162389.

Machiavelli, N. (1950). *The Prince*. New York: Random House. (Original work published 1532.)

Marton, F. (1988). Describing and improving teaching. In R. R. Schmeck (Ed.), *Learning strategies and learning styles*. New York: Plenum.

Marton, F. & Saljo, R. (1976). On qualitative differences in learning: I - Outcome and process. *British Journal of Educational Psychology*, 46, 4–11.

McCarthy, J. W., Smith, J. L. & DeLuca, D. (2010). Using online discussion boards with large and small groups to enhance learning of assistive technology. *Journal of Computing in Higher Education*, 22, 95–113.

McLuhan, M. (1995). *Understanding media: The extensions of man*. Cambridge, MA: MIT Press.

Means, B., Toyama, Y., Murphy, R., Bakia, M. & Jones, K. (2009). Evaluation of evidence-based practices in online learning: A meta-analysis and review of online learning studies. U.S. Department of Education. Retrieved July 29, 2010 from http://www2.ed.gov/rschstat/eval/tech/evidence-based-practices/finalreport.pdf.

Meyer, K. (2003). Face-to-face versus threaded discussions: The role of time and higher-order thinking. *Journal of Asynchronous Learning Networks*, 7(3), 55–65.

Meyer, K. (2004). Evaluating Online Discussions: Four Difference Frames of Analysis. *Journal of Asynchronous Learning Networks*, 8(2), 101–114.

Miller, G. E. (2010). Collaboration versus competition: trends in online learning for workforce development. Retrieved July 29, 2010 from http://www.aln.org/node/2350.

National Center for Academic Transformation (see: http://www.thencat.org/).

Nippard, E. & Murphy, E. (2007). Social presence in the web-based synchronous secondary classroom. *Canadian Journal of Learning and Technology*, 33(1). Retrieved July 29, 2010 from http://www.cjlt.ca/index.php/cjlt/article/view/24/22.

Olson, D. K. (1994). *The world on paper: The conceptual and cognitive implications of reading and writing*. New York: Cambridge University Press.

Ong, W. (1982). *Orality and literacy*. New York: Routledge.

Paechter, M., Maier, B. & Macher, D. (2010). Students' expectations of and experiences in e-learning: Their relation to learning achievements and course satisfaction. *Computers and Education*, 54(1), 222–229.

Palloff, R. M. & Pratt, K. (2005). *Collaborating online: Learning together in community*. San Francisco: Jossey-Bass.

Palloff, R. M. & Pratt, K. (2009). *Assessing the online learner*. San Francisco: Jossey-Bass.

Paulsen, M. (1995). Moderating educational computer conferences. In Z. Berge & M. Collins (Eds.), *Computer Mediated Communication and the Online Classroom* (pp. 81–90). Cresskill, NJ: Hampton Press, Inc.

Pawan, F., Paulus, T. M., Yalcin, S. & Chang, C. F. (2003). Online learning: Patterns of engagement and interaction among in-service teachers. *Language Learning and Technology*, 7(3), 119–140.

Perry, B. & Edwards, M. (2005). Exemplary online educators: Creating a community of inquiry. *Turkish Online Journal of Distance Education*, 6(2), 46–54.

Peters, O. (2000). Digital learning environments: New possibilities and opportunities. *International Review of Research in Open and Distance Learning*, 1(1). Retrieved July 29, 2010 from http://www.irrodl.org/index.php/irrodl/article/view/3/23.

Peters, O. (2007). The most industrialized form of education. In M. G. Moore (Ed.), *Handbook of distance education* (pp. 57–68). Mahwah, NJ: Lawrence Erlbaum.

Piper, M. (2008). A five-step program for change. *University Affairs*, October 6.

Pisutova-Gerber, K. & Malovicova, J. (2009). Critical and higher order thinking in online threaded discussions in the Slovak context. *International Review of Research in Open and Distance Learning*, 10(1). Retrieved July 29, 2010 from http://www.irrodl.org/index.php/irrodl/article/view/589/1175.

Pittinsky, M. S. (2003). *The wired tower: Perspectives on the impact of the Internet on higher education*. NJ: Prentice Hall.

Power, M. & Vaughan, N. (2010). Redesigning online learning for international graduate seminar delivery. *Journal of Distance Education*, 24(2), 19–38.

Pratt, D. D. (1981). The dynamics of continuing education learning groups. *Canadian Journal of University Continuing Education*, 8(1), 26–32.

Privateer, P. M. (1999). Academic technology and the future of higher education. *The Journal of Higher Education*, 70(1), 60–79.

Ramsden, P. (1988). Context and strategy: Situational influences on learning. In R. R. Schmeck (Ed.), *Learning strategies and learning styles* (pp. 159–184). New York: Plenum.

Ramsden, P. (2003). *Learning to teach in higher education* (2nd edn.). London: Routledge.

Report of a University of Illinois Faculty Seminar, (1999). Teaching at an Internet distance: The pedagogy of online teaching and learning. Chicago: University of

Illinois. Retrieved July 29, 2010 from http://www.elc.uzh.ch/service/kursentwicklung/mediothek/literaturtipps/tid-final-12-5.pdf.

Resnick, L. B. (1987). *Education and learning to think*. Washington, DC: National Academy Press.

Richardson, J. C. & Ice, P. (2010). Investigating students' level of critical thinking across instructional strategies in online discussions. *Internet and Higher Education*, 13(1–2), 52–59.

Roblyer, M. D., Freeman, J., Donaldson, M. B. & Maddox, M. (2007). A comparison of outcomes of virtual school courses offered in synchronous and asynchronous formats. *The Internet and Higher Education*, 10(4), 261–268.

Roblyer, M. D., McDaniel, M., Webb, M., Herman, J. & Witty, J. V. (2010). Findings on Facebook in higher education: A comparison of college faculty and student uses and perceptions of social networking sites. *Internet and Higher Education*, 13, 134–140.

Rogers, P. & Lea, M. (2005). Social presence in distributed group environments: The role of social identity. *Behavior & Information Technology*, 24(2), 151–158.

Rosenberg, M. J. (2001). *E-learning: Strategies for delivering knowledge in the digital age*. New York: McGraw-Hill.

Rossman, M. (1999). Successful online teaching using an asynchronous learner discussion Forum. *Journal of Asynchronous Learning Network*, 3(2), 91–97.

Rourke, L. & Anderson, T. (2002). Exploring social communication in computer conferencing. *Journal of Interactive Learning Research*, 13(3), 259–275.

Rourke, L., Anderson, T., Archer, W. and Garrison, D. R. (1999). Assessing social presence in asynchronous, text-based computer conferences. *Journal of Distance Education*, 14(3), 51–70.

Rourke, L., Anderson, T., Garrison, R. & Archer, W. (2001). Methodological issues in the content analysis of computer conference transcripts. *International Journal of Artificial Intelligence in Education*, 12(1), 8–22.

Rourke, L. & Kanuka, H. (2007). Barriers to online discourse. *Computer Supported Collaborative Learning*, 2, 105–126.

Rourke, L. & Kanuka, H. (2009). Learning in communities of inquiry: A review of the literature. *Journal of Distance Education*, 23(1), 19–48.

Rovai, A. P. (2002). Building sense of community at a distance. *International Review of Research in Open and Distance Education*, 3(1). Retrieved July 29, 2010 from http://www.irrodl.org/index.php/irrodl/article/view/79/153.

Rovai, A. P. & Jordan, H. M. (2004). Blended learning and sense of community: A comparative analysis with traditional and fully online graduate courses. *International Review of Research in Open and Distance Education*, 5(2). Retrieved July 29, 2010 from http://www.irrodl.org/index.php/irrodl/article/view/192/795

Rowntree, D. (1977). *Assessing students*. London: Harper & Row.

Sanger, L. (2010). Individual knowledge in the Internet age. *EDUCAUSE Review*, 45(2), 14–24.

Schellens, T., Van Keer, H., De Wever, B. & Valcke, M. (2009). Tagging thinking types in asynchronous discussion groups: Effects on critical thinking. *Interactive Learning Environments*, 17(1), 77–94.

Schrage, M. (1989). *No more teams! Mastering the dynamics of creative collaboration*. New York: Currency Doubleday.

Schreiner, L. A. (2009). *Linking student satisfaction with retention*. Retrieved July

29, 2010 from https://www.noellevitz.com/NR/rdonlyres/A22786EF-65FF-4053-A15A-CBE145B0C708/0/LinkingStudentSatis0809.pdf.

Schrire, S. (2004). Interaction and cognition in asynchronous computer conferencing. *Instructional Science, 32,* 475–502.

Schrire, S. (2006). Knowledge building in asynchronous discussion groups: Going beyond quantitative analysis. *Computers & Education,* 46(1), 49–70.

Shea, P. & Bidjerano, T. (2009a). Community of inquiry as a theoretical framework to foster "epistemic engagement" and "cognitive presence" in online education. *Computers and Education,* 52(3), 543–553.

Shea, P. & Bidjerano, T. (2009b). Cognitive presence and online learner engagement: A cluster analysis of the community of inquiry framework. *Journal of Computing in Higher Education,* 21, 199–217.

Shea, P., Hayes, S., Vickers, J., Gozza-Cohen, M., Uzner, S., Mehta, R., Valchova, A. & Rangan, P. (2010). A re-examination of the community of inquiry framework: Social network and content analysis. *Internet and Higher Education,* 1–2, 10–21.

Shea, P., Li, C. S. & Pickett, A. (2006). A study of teaching presence and student sense of learning community in fully online and web-enhanced college courses. *The Internet and Higher Education,* 9(3), 175–190.

Short, J., Williams, E. & Christie, B. (1976). *The Social Psychology of Telecommunications.* Toronto: John Wiley and Sons.

Sims, R. (2001). From art to alchemy: Achieving success with online learning. *IT Forum,* 55. Retrieved June 6, 2002 from http://it.coe.uga.edu/itforum/paper55.htm

So, H. & Brush, T. A. (2008). Student perceptions of collaborative learning, social presence and satisfaction in a blended learning environment: Relationships and critical factors. *Computers & Education,* 51(1), 318–336.

Staley, J. & Ice, P. (2009). *Instructional design project management 2.0: A model of development and practice.* Paper presented at the 25th Annual Conference on Distance Teaching and Learning, Madison, WI, August.

Stein, D. (1992) (Ed.). *Cooperating with written texts: The pragmatics and comprehension of written texts.* Berlin: Mouton de Gruyter.

Stein, D. S., Wanstreet, C. E., Glazer, H. R., Engle, C. L. Harris, R. A., Johnston, S. M., Simons, M. R. & Trinko, L. A. (2007). Creating shared understanding through chats in a community of inquiry. *The Internet and Higher Education,* 10, 103–115.

Swan, K. & Ice, P. (2010) Special issue on the Community of Inquiry framework: Ten years later. *The Internet and Higher Education,* 13(1–2), pp. 1–100.

Swan, K. & Richardson, J. C. (2003). Examining social presence in online courses in relation to students' perceived learning and satisfaction. *Journal of Asynchronous Learning Networks,* 7, 68–82.

Swan, K., Schenker, J., Arnold, S. & Kuo, C.-L. (2007). Shaping online discussion: assessment matters. *e-Mentor,* 1(18), 78–82.

Swan, K., Shen, J. & Hiltz, R. (2006). Assessment and collaboration in online learning. *Journal of Asynchronous Learning Networks,* 10(1), 45–62.

Tapscott, D. (1996). *The digital economy: Promise and peril in the age of networked intelligence.* NY: McGraw-Hill.

Tapscott, D. & Williams, A. D. (2010). Innovating the 21st-century university: It's time. *EDUCAUSE Review,* 45(1), 16–29.

Twigg, C. A. (2003). Improving learning and reducing costs: New models for online learning. *EDUCAUSE Review*, 38(5), 29–38.

Valcke, M., De Wever, B., Zhu, C. & Deed, C. (2009). Supporting active cognitive processing in collaborative groups: Potential of Bloom's taxonomy as a labelling tool. *Internet and Higher Education*, 12, 165–172.

Vaughan, N. & Garrison, D. R. (2005). Creating cognitive presence in a blended faculty development community. *Internet and Higher Education*, 8(1), 1–12.

Vaughan, N. & Garrison, D. R. (2006). How blended learning can support a faculty community of inquiry. *Journal of Asynchronous Learning Networks*, 10(4), 139–152.

Walther, J. (1992). Interpersonal effects in computer mediated interaction: A relational perspective. *Communication Research*, 19(1), 52–90.

Weigel, V. B. (2002). *Deep learning for a digital age: technology's untapped potential to enrich higher education*. San Francisco: Jossey-Bass.

Wells, G. (1999). *Dialogic Inquiry*. Cambridge: Cambridge University Press.

Yeh, S. S. (2009). The cost-effectiveness of raising teacher quality. *Educational Research Review*, 4(3), 220–232.

Young, A. & Fry, J. D. (2008). Metacognitive awareness and academic achievement in college students. *Journal of the Scholarship of Teaching and Learning*, 8(2), 1–10.

Index

THIRD EDITION

e Moder@ting

THE KEY TO TEACHING AND LEARNING ONLINE

GILLY SALMON

Professor Gilly Salmon has achieved continuity
and illumination of the seminal five stage model,
together with new research-based developments,
in her much-awaited third edition of
E-Moderating—the most quoted and successful
guide for e-learning practitioners.

Never content to offer superficial revisions
or simple "solutions" against the pace of
technological advances, the expanding interest
and requirements for online learning, and the
changes they have wrought, *E-Moderating-3*
offers a richness of applied topics that will
directly impact learners and teachers of all kinds.
The book is carefully crafted and supported with
evidence, examples, and resources for practical
guidelines, making it potentially transformational
for all practitioners.

E-Moderating-3 includes:

- Updates of literature, key terms, case
  studies and projects

- Fresh examples of the use of the five stage
  model around the world, at different levels
  of education and across disciplines

- Guidelines for moderating for podcasting
  and virtual worlds

- Illustrations from the latest All Things in
  Moderation development programmes
  (www.atimod.com)

- New resources for practitioners

Book Web Site: **www.e-moderating.com**

June 2011: 240pp
Pb: 978-0-415-88174-6
Hb: 978-0-415-88173-9
eBook: 978-0-203-81668-4

View Inside
Online

Routledge
Taylor & Francis Group

Routledge... think about it
www.routledge.com/education

Essentials of Online Course Design

A Standards-Based Guide

Marjorie Vai and **Kristen Sosulski**

Essentials of Online Course Design takes a fresh, thoughtfully designed, step-by-step approach to online course development. At its core is a set of standards that are based on best practices in the field of online learning and teaching. Pedagogical, organizational and visual design principles are presented and modeled throughout the book and users will quickly learn from the guide's hands-on approach. The course design process begins with the elements of a classroom syllabus which, after a series of guided steps, easily evolve into an online course outline.

The guide's key features include:

- a practical approach informed by theory
- clean interior design that offers straightforward guidance from page one
- clear and jargon-free language
- examples, screen shots, and illustrations to clarify and support the text
- a Companion Website with examples, adaptable templates, interactive learning features, and online resources
- a checklist of online course design standards that readers can use to self-evaluate.

Essentials of Online Course Design serves as a best-practice model for designing online courses. After reading this book, readers will find that preparing for online teaching is, contrary to popular belief, a satisfying and engaging experience. The core issue is simply good design: pedagogical, organizational, and visual.

January 2011: 204pp
Pb: 978-0-415-87300-0
Hb: 978-0-415-87299-7
eBook: 978-0-203-83831-0

View Inside Online

Routledge
Taylor & Francis Group

Routledge... think about it
www.routledge.com/education

Routledge Resources for
Teaching in Higher Education

The one stop shop for your teaching needs!

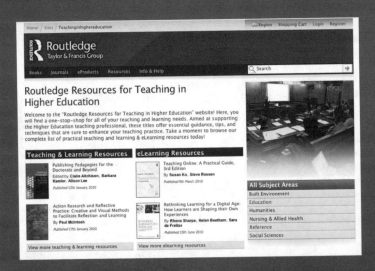

Aimed at supporting the Higher Education teaching professional, this website highlights books that offer essential guidance, tips, and techniques that are sure to enhance your teaching practice.

Take a moment to browse our complete list of practical teaching and learning & eLearning resources today!

www.routledge.com/teachinginhighereducation